LIFE PICTURE PUZZLE

WELCOME TO LIFE'S THIRD PICTURE PUZZLE BOOK

To those of you who have been with us from the beginning: Welcome back! And to anyone joining us for the first time: Nice to meet you. Didn't we warn you about the somewhat addictive nature of these puzzles? Oh, well, it couldn't hurt you to try just one.

After we published the second Picture Puzzle book, we were overwhelmed by the positive response, just as we were after the first—letters, e-mails, phone calls in the middle of the night. And just as we did after the first book, we decided to create something truly special for the next edition. We've increased the number of differences to search for throughout the book to maximize your pleasure per page. We've also added a new category of puzzles: animals. (These aren't any easier or harder than the rest, just furrier.) And if you thought the previous Picture Puzzle books were perfect, don't worry: All your favorite types of puzzles are still here.

More good news: The fourth LIFE Picture Puzzle book is already in the works. Should this edition fail to tide you over until the next one appears, check out our online archive of puzzles at *www.LIFE.com*. If you want to let us know what you think of the new book, drop us a line at picturepuzzle@life.com. We'd love to hear from you.

[OUR CUT-UP PUZZLES: EASY AS 1-2-3]

We snipped a photo into 4, 6, 12, or 16 pieces. Then we rearranged the pieces and numbered them.

Your mission: Beneath each cut-up puzzle, write the number of the piece in the box where it belongs.

Check the answer key at the back of the book to see what the reassembled image looks like.

Secret puzzle bonus! We've concealed 10 secret changes in the puzzles within this book. Think you've found one? Log on to *www.LIFE.com/Life/extra_answers* to find out! In addition, we've hidden two more puzzles on our Web site, but you can reach them only through the private entrance: Go to *www.LIFE.com*, and click PICTURE PUZZLE. On the next page, click the second *Z* in the word PUZZLE, close your eyes, count to three, and voilà!

[HOW TO PLAY THE PUZZLES]

Make a Splash
Wake up and note the changes to this backyard balloon party

The puzzle's difficulty rating; this one is a master, or an intermediate level.

9
changes
- - - - - - -
KEEP SCORE

The number of changes we've made to the original photograph. Remember, we've also hidden a *secret*, uncounted difference in 10 of the puzzles.

2min 45sec

The suggested time in which to finish the puzzle— for competitive puzzlers only.

Answers on page 166

SUPERSTOCK, INC./SUPERSTOCK

The differences between pictures can range from the relatively obvious to the maddeningly subtle, depending on the difficulty rating. For instance, here, now Dad's shirt has his yearly ranking on it, and there is a patch of sunflowers in the bushes. Seven more changes are left to spot in this one.

The page on which the answers can be found. Use the numbered and lettered grid to help you find any changes you might have missed.

LIFE PICTURE PUZZLE

Editor Mark Adams
Deputy Editor Maura Fritz
Production Manager Michael Roseman
Research Editor Danny Freedman

LIFE Puzzle Books
Managing Editor Bill Shapiro
Creative Director Richard Baker

LIFE Books
President Andrew Blau
Business Manager Roger Adler
Business Development Manager Jeff Burak
Editorial Director Robert Sullivan

Editorial Operations Richard K. Prue, David Sloan (DIRECTORS), Richard Shaffer (GROUP MANAGER), Burt Carnesi, Brian Fellows, Raphael Joa, Angel Mass, Stanley E. Moyse (MANAGERS), Soheila Asayesh, Keith Aurelio, Trang Ba Chuong, Ellen Bohan, Charlotte Coco, Osmar Escalona, Kevin Hart, Norma Jones, Mert Kerimoglu, Rosalie Khan, Marco Lau, Po Fung Ng, Rudi Papiri, Barry Pribula, Carina A. Rosario, Albert Rufino, Christopher Scala, Diana Suryakusuma, Vaune Trachtman, Paul Tupay, Lionel Vargas, David Weiner

Produced by

DOWNTOWN
BOOKWORKS INC.

President Julie Merberg
Editor and Photo Researcher Sarah Parvis

Special thanks to Patty Brown, Sara Newberry, Kate Gibson, Brian Michael Thomas, Andrew James Capelli

Puzzle Photo Manipulation Reddish-Blue Inc.

Time Inc. Home Entertainment
Publisher Richard Fraiman
General Manager Steven Sandonato
Executive Director, Marketing Services Carol Pittard
Director, Retail & Special Sales Tom Mifsud
Director, New Product Development Peter Harper
Assistant Director, Brand Marketing Laura Adam
Assistant General Counsel Dasha Smith Dwin
Book Production Manager Jonathan Polsky
Manager, Prepress & Design Anne-Michelle Gallero

Special thanks to Bozena Bannett, Alexandra Bliss, Glenn Buonocore, Suzanne Janso, Robert Marasco, Brooke McGuire, Mary Sarro-Waite, Ilene Schreider, Adriana Tierno, Alex Voznesenskiy

PUBLISHED BY

LIFE BOOKS

Vol. 7, No. 5 • August 2007

If you would like to order any of our hardcover Collector's Edition books, please call us at 800-327-6388 (Monday through Friday, 7 a.m. to 8 p.m., or Saturday, 7 a.m. to 6 p.m. Central Time). Please visit us, and sample past editions of LIFE, at *www.LIFE.com.*

READY, SET,

GO!

These puzzles are for everyone:
rookies and veterans,
young and old. Start here, and
sharpen your skills.

Farm Team

These little fellas solved this one. Can you?

A

B

C

D

E

1   2   3   4   5

10
changes
- - - - - - - - -
KEEP
SCORE

3min 25sec

Answers
on page 166

Made in the Shade

It'll be hard to top this

A

B

C

D

E

1 | 2 | 3 | 4 | 5

10
changes
- - - - - - - - -
KEEP
SCORE

❏
❏
❏
❏
❏
❏
❏
❏
❏
❏

⧗

2min 40sec

Answers
on page 166

Getting Crafty

Keep your eyes glued to the shapes, and you're sure to make the cut

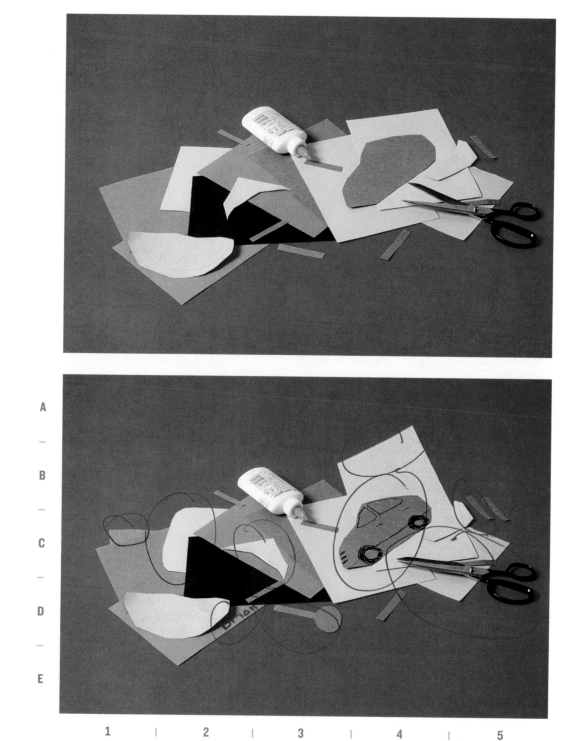

9
changes

- - - - - - - -

KEEP
SCORE

☐
☐
☐
☐
☐
☐
☐
☐
☐

⧖

2min 30sec

Answers
on page 166

A
—
B
—
C
—
D
—
E

1   2   3   4   5

Hook, Line, and Sinker

Good luck tackling this puzzle

9
changes

KEEP
SCORE

3min 30sec

Answers
on page 166

Double Vision

Some redecorating can definitely be seen here

12
changes

- - - - - - - -

KEEP
SCORE

❏
❏
❏
❏
❏
❏
❏
❏
❏
❏
❏
❏

⧗

2min 45sec

Answers
on page 166

A
—
B
—
C
—
D
—
E

1 | 2 | 3 | 4 | 5

AGE FOTOSTOCK/SUPERSTOCK

Simple Directions

No clue about how to get to Gnome, though

Answers
on page 166

10 changes

KEEP SCORE

3min 20sec

It's a Scorcher

You're on a hot streak—don't stop now

A

B

C

D

E

1   2   3   4   5

9
changes
- - - - - - - -
KEEP
SCORE

❏
❏
❏
❏
❏
❏
❏
❏
❏

⌛

2min 10sec

Answers
on page 166

Along Came a Spider

Stay calm. Sharpen your pencil. And get to work.

A

—

B

—

C

—

D

—

E

1 | 2 | 3 | 4 | 5

8
changes

- - - - - - - -

KEEP
SCORE

❏
❏
❏
❏
❏
❏
❏
❏

⌛

2min 25sec

Answers
on page 166

Petals Pushed

These floral arrangements may be equally lovely,
but they're not quite identical

FLOWER POWER

A

B

C

D

E

1   2   3   4   5

12
changes
- - - - - - - -
KEEP
SCORE

4min 15sec

Answers
on page 167

Extra! Extra!

A puzzle this sneaky should be front-page news. Check out
what's happened since the early edition.

10
changes

KEEP
SCORE

❑ ❑
❑
❑ ❑
❑
❑ ❑
❑
❑ ❑

⏳

3min 0sec

Answers
on page 167

A

—

B

—

C

—

D

—

E

1   2   3   4   5

All Ears

Make no bones about it:
This puzzle is *ruff!*

A

B

C

D

E

1   2   3   4   5

9
changes

KEEP
SCORE

⌛

3min 50sec

Answers
on page 167

Focus on the Present

Here's a small gift: A couple of the differences between
these photos are merely ornamental

A

B

C

D

E

1   2   3   4   5

10
changes

KEEP
SCORE

❏
❏
❏
❏
❏
❏
❏
❏
❏
❏

⧗
2min 55sec

Answers
on page 167

I Do!

One of these couples is feeling blue.
Which is not like the rest?

1

2

3

4

5

6

0min 25sec

Answer
on page 167

If the Shoe Fits . . .

. . . wear it. But one size does not fit all.
A pair of kicks is hiding something.

1

2

3

4

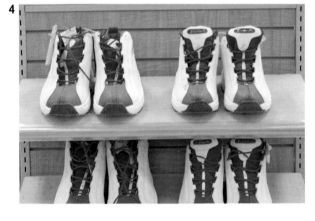

5

6

0min 35sec

Answer
on page 167

Hats? Sure. Hard? Nah.

This one was built especially for you

A

B

C

D

E

1 | 2 | 3 | 4 | 5

10
changes
- - - - - - - - -
KEEP
SCORE

❏
❏
❏
❏
❏
❏
❏
❏
❏
❏

⌛

2min 50sec

Answers
on page 167

Color Blocks

We cut up this snapshot and scrambled the pieces.
Can you help sort out the squares?

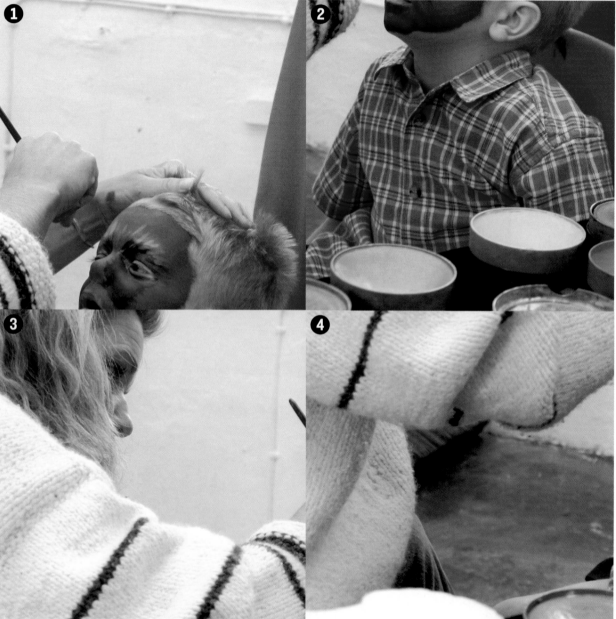

GARY COOK/ALAMY

⧗
0min 40sec

Answer
on page 167

KEEP SCORE

This Does Not Compute

Things went a little haywire here.
Use the chart below to reassemble the laptop lounger.

KEEP SCORE

0min 25sec

Answer
on page 167

What Up, Dawg?

Or, wait, should that be *dawgs*?

SCHOOL ZONE

A

B

C

D

E

1   2   3   4   5

11
changes

- - - - - - - -

KEEP
SCORE

2min 40sec

Answers
on page 167

Get Ready to Order

A few things are out of place
in this deserted diner

10
changes

KEEP
SCORE

4min 10sec

Answers
on page 167

A

B

C

D

E

1   2   3   4   5

Mug Shot

These cabinets are filled to the rim
with sneaky differences

10
changes

- - - - - - - - -

KEEP
SCORE

3min 55sec

Answers
on page 168

Tiptoe Through the Treetops

The leaves may not be turning yet, but other
arboreal changes are afoot

11
changes

KEEP
SCORE

A

B

C

D

E

⌛

4min 0sec

Answers
on page 168

1   2   3   4   5

AGE FOTOSTOCK/SUPERSTOCK

Can You Dig It?

Don't let your skills get rusty—you'll soon see
how the shovels are shifting

A
—
B
—
C
—
D
—
E

1   2   3   4   5

10
changes
- - - - - - - - -
KEEP
SCORE

⏳

3min 40sec

Answers
on page 168

It's a Grand Old Flag

These patriotic princesses are celebrating in style with their stars and stripes.
Can you spot the newest all-American trends?

10
changes
- - - - - - - - -
KEEP
SCORE

❑ ❑ ❑ ❑ ❑ ❑ ❑ ❑ ❑

⧗

3min 15sec

Answers
on page 168

Game, Set, Match

Think you know the score? Well, then,
the ball's in your court.

9
changes
- - - - - - - - -
KEEP
SCORE
❏
❏
❏
❏
❏
❏
❏
❏
❏

⧗

2min 5sec

Answers
on page 168

Of Mice and Man

This one is destined to be a classic

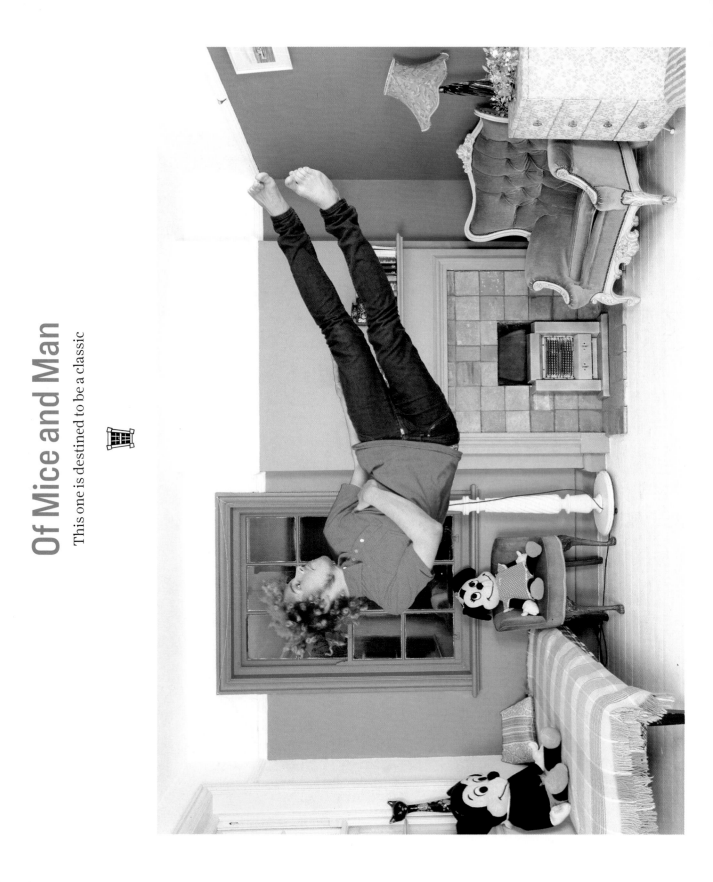

20
changes

- - - - - - - - -

KEEP
SCORE

6min 20sec

Answers
on page 168

ER[

Here, puzzles get
a little harder. You'll
need to raise
your game a level.

Key Quest

A pro like you should have this puzzle
buttoned up in a snap

A

B

C

D

E

1   2   3   4   5

12
changes
- - - - - - - - -
KEEP
SCORE

☐
☐
☐
☐
☐
☐
☐
☐
☐
☐
☐
☐

⌛

4min 20sec

Answers
on page 168

It's in the Bag

Someone has to shoulder the burden of solving this puzzle.
Will you?

9
changes

- - - - - - - - -

KEEP
SCORE

❏
❏
❏
❏
❏
❏
❏
❏
❏

⧗

3min 50sec

Answers
on page 168

A

—

B

—

C

—

D

—

E

1   2   3   4   5

AGE FOTOSTOCK/SUPERSTOCK

Tidying Up

A few messy inconsistencies are hiding in
this home's modern conveniences

A

—

B

—

C

—

D

—

E

1 | 2 | 3 | 4 | 5

10
changes

KEEP
SCORE

❏
❏
❏
❏
❏
❏
❏
❏
❏
❏

⌛

3min 25sec

Answers
on page 168

Off-Kilter

Someone redesigned the prints and plaids here

12
changes

KEEP
SCORE

☐
☐
☐
☐
☐
☐
☐
☐
☐
☐
☐
☐

⌛

4min 30sec

Answers
on page 169

A
—
B
—
C
—
D
—
E

1   2   3   4   5

DON B. STEVENSON/ALAMY

Rain Delay

Better hurry—looks like it's going to pour

13
changes
- - - - - - -
KEEP
SCORE

❏
❏
❏
❏
❏
❏
❏
❏
❏
❏
❏
❏
❏

⧗

3min 55sec

Answers
on page 169

Chilly Dogs

This pack had no trouble sniffing out the alterations we made. Now it's your turn.

SLEIGH BELLS RING

A
B
C
D
E

1   2   3   4   5

11
changes

KEEP
SCORE

☐ ☐ ☐ ☐ ☐ ☐ ☐ ☐ ☐ ☐ ☐

⧗

5min 35sec

Answers
on page 169

Pretty in Pink

This one really seems like your cup of tea. Now,
if only the pastries would stay put.

10
changes

KEEP
SCORE

4min 0sec

Answers
on page 169

A

B

C

D

E

1   2   3   4   5

Rake It In

With all this yard equipment, anyone can get
a handle on stray changes

A
—
B
—
C
—
D
—
E

1   2   3   4   5

11
changes
- - - - - -
KEEP
SCORE

⌛

4min 30sec

Answers
on page 169

Liquid Assets

The prices are moving in the cleaning aisle. The question is:
Which way are they going?

11
changes

- - - - - - - - -

KEEP
SCORE

❑
❑
❑
❑
❑
❑
❑
❑
❑
❑
❑

⧗

4min 15sec

Answers
on page 169

A

B

C

D

E

1 | 2 | 3 | 4 | 5

'Tis the Season . . .

. . . to pull out the winter decorations and see
if everything's in order (hint: It's not)

A

B

C

D

E

1 | 2 | 3 | 4 | 5

11
changes

KEEP
SCORE

❏
❏
❏
❏
❏
❏
❏
❏
❏
❏
❏

⧗

3min 45sec

Answers
on page 169

Another Bloomin' Puzzle

Some odd things are popping up in his garden

14
changes

- - - - - - - -

KEEP
SCORE

☑
☑
☑
☑
☑
☑
☑
☑
☑
☑
☑
☑
☑
☐

⌛

5min 40sec

Answers
on page 169

A
—
B
—
C
—
D
—
E

1 | 2 | 3 | 4 | 5

Housing Crunch

Every day is moving day in this neighborhood

A

B

C

D

E

1   2   3   4   5

10
changes

KEEP
SCORE

☐
☐
☐
☐
☐
☐
☐
☐
☐

⧖

6min 30sec

Answers
on page 169

Honk if You Spot It

Five of these photos are identical. One has been altered.
Which is the impostor?

1

2

3

4

5

6

1min 20sec

Answer
on page 170

Patio Daddy-O

The retro cookouts below may all look the same, but one backyard barbecue is unique. Can you find it?

1

2

3

4

5

6

0min 45sec

Answer
on page 170

Quantum Leap

It's just a hop, skip, and a jump from one photo to the next.
How did so many things change?

A

–

B

–

C

–

D

–

E

1 | 2 | 3 | 4 | 5

10
changes
- - - - - - - - -
KEEP
SCORE

❏
❏
❏
❏
❏
❏
❏
❏
❏
❏

⧗
———
4min 15sec

Answers
on page 170

Bumper Crop

Try to pick out the mess of differences

11
changes
- - - - - - -
KEEP
SCORE

❏
❏
❏
❏
❏
❏
❏
❏
❏
❏
❏

⧖
6 min 5 sec

Answers
on page 170

A | B | C | D | E

1 2 3 4 5

Are You Ready to Rock?

'Cause you're on a *roll*, baby!

A

B

C

D

E

1 | 2 | 3 | 4 | 5

11
changes
- - - - - - - - -
KEEP
SCORE

❏
❏
❏
❏
❏
❏
❏
❏
❏
❏
❏

⌛

3min 40sec

Answers
on page 170

Inner Peace

Meditate on the imbalances in these two photos

10
changes

- - - - - - - - -

KEEP
SCORE

⏳

4min 30sec

Answers
on page 170

A
—
B
—
C
—
D
—
E

1 | 2 | 3 | 4 | 5

Quit Clowning Around

This puzzle is packed with changes

11 changes

KEEP SCORE

5min 20sec

Answers on page 170

Think Outside the Lines

Some artists tinker with their work until it is *just* right.
Check out this Rembrandt's most recent revisions.

A

—

B

—

C

—

D

—

E

1 | 2 | 3 | 4 | 5

9
changes
- - - - - - - - -
KEEP
SCORE

❏
❏
❏
❏
❏
❏
❏
❏
❏

⧗

3min 45sec

Answers
on page 170

Bedroom Brainteaser

Things are shifting around this tidy room

11
changes

- - - - - - - -

KEEP
SCORE

☐ ☐
☐ ☐
☐ ☐
☐ ☐
☐ ☐
☐

⏳

5min 25sec

Answers
on page 170

A

—

B

—

C

—

D

—

E

1 | 2 | 3 | 4 | 5

Wash and Go

Hey, get back there! This puzzle isn't finished!

A
—
B
—
C
—
D
—
E

1 | 2 | 3 | 4 | 5

9
changes
- - - - - - - -
KEEP
SCORE

❏
❏
❏
❏
❏
❏
❏
❏
❏

⌛

4min 50sec

Answers
on page 170

Everything Must Go

Use the boxes at the bottom to put this business in its place.
Its proper place, that is.

1min 35sec

Answer
on page 171

KEEP SCORE

Snail Mail

We snipped this snapshot into pieces. Can you put
the rusty wheels back together again?

KEEP SCORE

⧗

1min 15sec

Answer
on page 171

Bowled Over

Some paint won't stop running. Find the flowers
that are getting out of line.

A

—

B

—

C

—

D

—

E

1   2   3   4   5

10
changes

KEEP
SCORE

❏
❏
❏
❏
❏
❏
❏
❏
❏
❏

⧗
5min 25sec

Answers
on page 171

Meow Mix-ups

Kitty's garden is growing and changing.
Can you dig up the differences?

10
changes

- - - - - - -

KEEP
SCORE

5min 40sec

Answers
on page 171

A

—

B

—

C

—

D

—

E

1   2   3   4   5

AGE FOTOSTOCK/SUPERSTOCK

The Bar Is Raised

Ingredients have been shaken, stirred,
swapped, and shifted. Cheers!

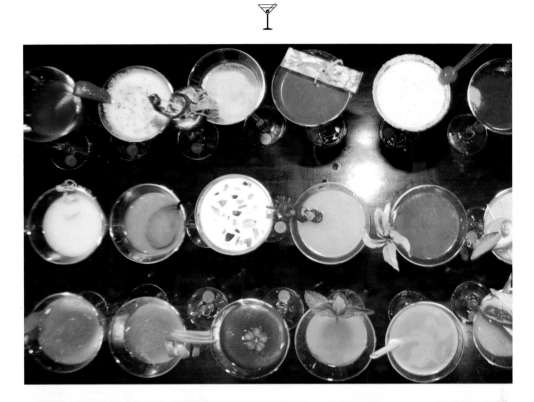

A

—

B

—

C

—

D

—

E

1 | 2 | 3 | 4 | 5

10
changes

- - - - - - - -

KEEP
SCORE

❏
❏
❏
❏
❏
❏
❏
❏
❏
❏

⧗

4min 30sec

Answers
on page 171

Hunting Party

These three musketeers are hiding something

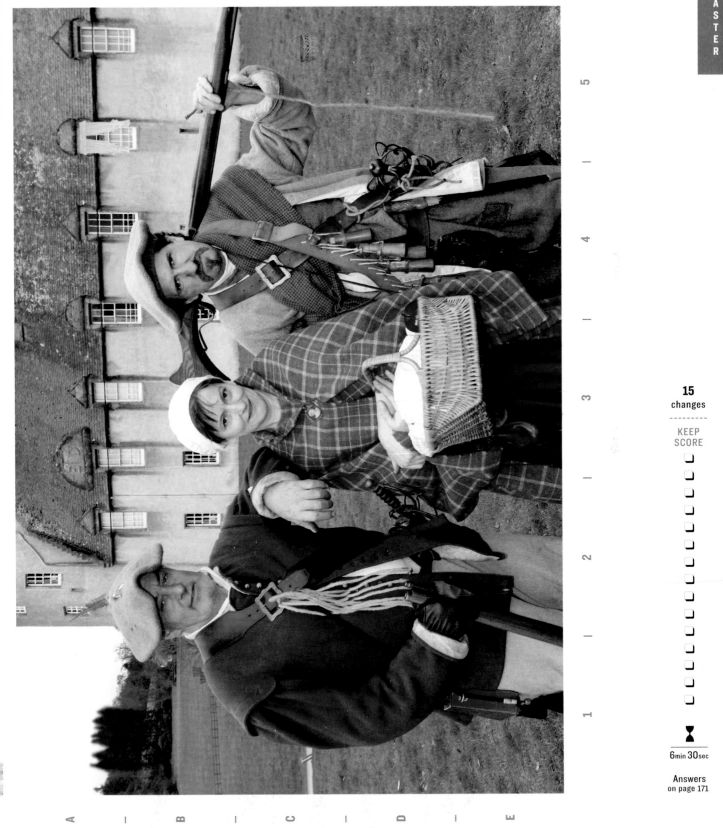

5   4   3   2   1

A   B   C   D   E

15
changes

KEEP
SCORE

⌛
6min 30sec

Answers
on page 171

RT [

Only serious puzzlers
dare to tread past this point.
Who's in?

]

Market Madness

There are bushels of fun to be had plucking the differences
out of these fruity photos

A

B

C

D

E

1 | 2 | 3 | 4 | 5

10
changes
- - - - - - - - -
KEEP
SCORE

❏
❏
❏
❏
❏
❏
❏
❏
❏
❏

⧗

7min 10sec

Answers
on page 171

Gettin' Wiggy With It

Some tinting and snipping has occurred here, but you'll have to look twice to spot the differences

12
changes

KEEP
SCORE

⏳
12min **25**sec

Answers
on page 171

A
—
B
—
C
—
D
—
E

1   2   3   4   5

Notes From a Marriage

The couple that plays together stays together.
You folks like puzzles?

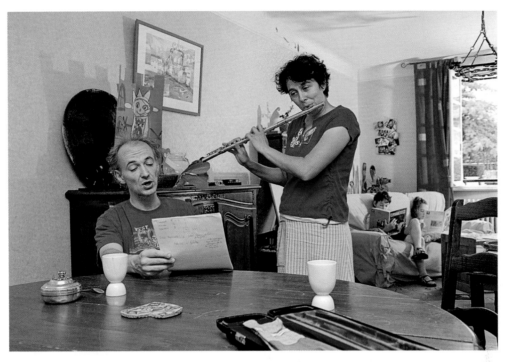

A
—
B
—
C
—
D
—
E

1 | 2 | 3 | 4 | 5

10
changes

KEEP
SCORE

❏
❏
❏
❏
❏
❏
❏
❏
❏
❏

⌛

6 min 50 sec

Answers
on page 171

Don't Lose Your Marbles

Might want to approach this with some circular logic

〉〉〉〉●●

A — B — C — D — E

1 | 2 | 3 | 4 | 5

10 changes

- - - - - - - - -

KEEP SCORE

❏
❏
❏
❏
❏
❏
❏
❏
❏
❏

⧗

10min 30sec

Answers on page 171

Island Breeze

This should be so easy for a pro like you

A

B

C

D

E

1   2   3   4   5

11
changes

KEEP
SCORE

❏
❏
❏
❏
❏
❏
❏
❏
❏
❏
❏

⧗

9min 15sec

Answers
on page 172

Over the Limit

The contents of these pictures may have shifted in transit

A

B

C

D

E

1   2   3   4   5

11
changes

KEEP
SCORE

❏
❏
❏
❏
❏
❏
❏
❏
❏
❏
❏

⧖
14min 20sec

Answers
on page 172

Distinctive Blend

We'd label a photo below as one-of-a-kind.
Which is it?

1

2

3

4

5

6

4min 50sec

Answer
on page 172

ALAIN COUILLAUD/ALAMY

Arcade Fun

One picture is different from the others.
Aim to find it.

1

2

3

4

5

6

3min 35sec

Answer
on page 172

Grill, Interrupted

This barbecue is all mixed up. Can you smoke out
the modifications to this family gathering?

11
changes

- - - - - - -

KEEP
SCORE

❏
❏
❏
❏
❏
❏
❏
❏
❏
❏
❏

⧗

8min 45sec

Answers
on page 172

Agony of the Feet

Choosing sandals is hard enough—but just try to choose
when the styles keep changing

11
changes

KEEP
SCORE

A

B

C

D

E

11min 5sec

Answers
on page 172

1   2   3   4   5

Autumn Serenade

That scarecrow sure can hit the high notes. See what else is worth singing about around here.

11
changes

- - - - - - - -

KEEP
SCORE

❏
❏
❏
❏
❏
❏
❏
❏
❏
❏
❏

⏳

11min 55sec

Answers
on page 172

Show of Hands

We did a little digital work on this photo

A

B

C

D

E

1   2   3   4   5

12
changes
- - - - - - - -
KEEP
SCORE
❏
❏
❏
❏
❏
❏
❏
❏
❏
❏
❏
❏

⏳
13min 10sec

Answers
on page 172

Read the Signs

Be sure to follow directions, or you'll go astray

11
changes

KEEP
SCORE

☐ ☐ ☐ ☐ ☐ ☐ ☐ ☐ ☐ ☐ ☐

⧖

8min 40sec

Answers
on page 172

All Tangoed Up

These two need a little help with their dance routine.
Can you straighten it out?

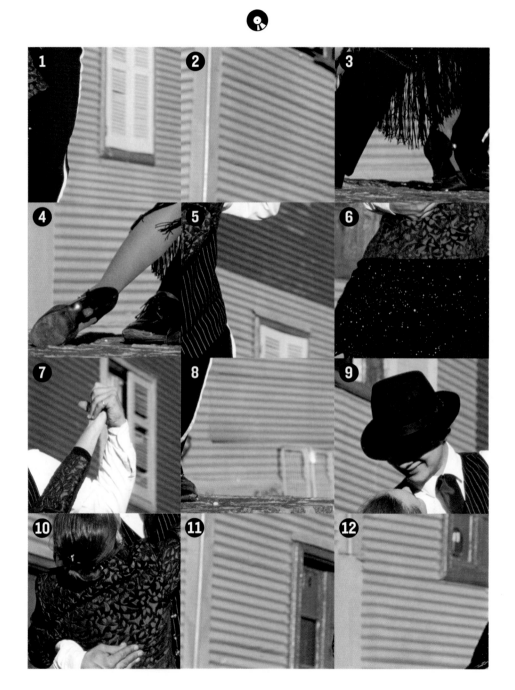

SERGIO PITAMITZ/ALAMY

3min 45sec

Answer
on page 172

KEEP SCORE

Window of Opportunity

You have the chance to set this scene right.
Use the grid below to replot it.

✿

Answer
on page 173

4min 50sec

KEEP SCORE

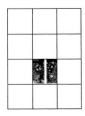

EXPERT

Boning Up

Be patient—this one requires some digging

12
changes

- - - - - - - -

KEEP
SCORE

☐
☐
☐
☐
☐
☐
☐
☐
☐
☐
☐
☐

⌛

10min **20**sec

Answers
on page 173

A

B

C

D

E

1   2   3   4   5

PETER CASOLINO/ALAMY

Surfin' Safari

Is everyone onboard?

13
changes

- - - - - - - - -

KEEP
SCORE

☐
☐
☐
☐
☐
☐
☐
☐
☐
☐
☐
☐
☐

⌛

13min 15sec

Answers
on page 173

Playing Hardball

We threw you a curve here. Care to take a swing?

A B C D E
1 2 3 4 5

13
changes
- - - - - - - - -
KEEP
SCORE

☐ ☐ ☐ ☐ ☐ ☐ ☐ ☐ ☐ ☐ ☐ ☐ ☐

⏳

14min 5sec

Answers
on page 173

Ring-a-Ding-Ding!

You'd need two pairs of hands to count all the tricky differences in these photos

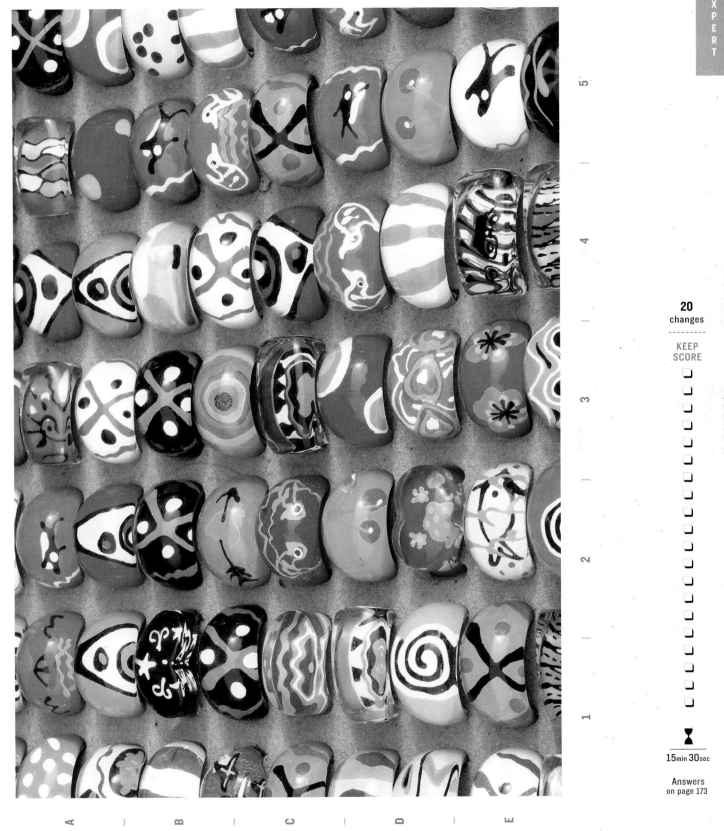

20
changes

- - - - - - - - -

KEEP
SCORE

☐
☐
☐
☐
☐
☐
☐
☐
☐
☐
☐
☐
☐
☐
☐
☐
☐
☐
☐
☐

⧗

15min 30sec

Answers
on page 173

5

4

3

2

1

A | B | C | D | E

All Dolled Up

How many wardrobe changes can you spy?

A

B

C

D

E

1   2   3   4   5

15
changes

KEEP
SCORE

❏
❏
❏
❏
❏
❏
❏
❏
❏
❏
❏
❏
❏
❏
❏

⧗

13min 55sec

Answers
on page 173

STEVE VIDLER/SUPERSTOCK

Not to Scale

For such a little fellow, he's made some big adjustments

11
changes

- - - - - - - - -

KEEP
SCORE

☐ ☐ ☐ ☐ ☐ ☐ ☐ ☐ ☐ ☐ ☐

⧗

9min 45sec

Answers
on page 173

A B C D E

1 2 3 4 5

Shuffled Cards

Greetings, seasoned puzzle veterans.
Be warned: This one's no holiday.

11
changes

KEEP
SCORE

⌛
14min 30sec

Answers
on page 173

A
B
C
D
E

1   2   3   4   5

City Slickers

Rain, rain, go away. Solve this puzzle,
and you deserve an A.

A
—
B
—
C
—
D
—
E

1   2   3   4   5

12
changes
- - - - - - - -
KEEP
SCORE

⌛
21min 15sec

Answers
on page 174

Lily Monster

Ponder this: It's possible the puzzle here is the most challenging yet

GENIUS

5

4

3

2

1

A

B

C

D

E

11
changes

KEEP
SCORE

⌛
18min 20sec

Answers
on page 174

Broken Window

Can you restore order to the garbled storefront?

⏳
8min 35sec

Answer
on page 174

KEEP SCORE

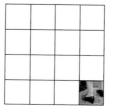

Just Your Type

Whoever solves this one gets a ribbon

KEEP SCORE

12min 40sec

Answer
on page 174

Pattern Mixing

This is one bizarre bazaar, where designs mysteriously change

12
changes

KEEP
SCORE

⧗
20min 50sec

Answers
on page 174

A | B | C | D | E

1   2   3   4   5

The Plane Truth

Fasten your seat belt, and expect some turbulence.
This one's definitely a white-knuckle flight.

5

4

20
changes
- - - - - - - - -
KEEP
SCORE

❏
❏
❏
❏
❏
❏
❏
❏
❏
❏
❏
❏
❏
❏
❏
❏
❏
❏
❏
❏

⌛

24min 0sec

Answers
on page 174

3

2

1

A   B   C   D   E

ROBBIE PLECK/SUPERSTOCK

JS[

Finding a single difference in these puzzles is a challenge. Finding them all might be impossible.

]

ALS[ ]

Here are puzzles
with a feature that's new:
Each one includes a
creature (or two).

Hang in There

What's this little guy all hopped up about?

A

—

B

—

C

—

D

—

E

1 | 2 | 3 | 4 | 5

10
changes

- - - - - - - -

KEEP
SCORE

2min 10sec

Answers
on page 174

Unusual Suspects

Apparently, all's not quite peaceful in the animal kingdom.
What changed in this lineup?

10
changes

KEEP
SCORE

2min 40sec

Answers
on page 174

A
—
B
—
C
—
D
—
E

1 | 2 | 3 | 4 | 5

Finding Nemo

More than fish are adrift in the aquarium.
Inspect the stones as well to catch *all* the changes.

10
changes
- - - - - - - -
KEEP
SCORE

A
—
B
—
C
—
D
—
E

1   2   3   4   5

3min 0sec

Answers
on page 174

Pretty Snaky

Dare we say it? Kind of a pain in the asp.

5

4

3

2

1

11
changes

- - - - - - - - -

KEEP
SCORE

☐
☐
☐
☐
☐
☐
☐
☐
☐
☐
☐

⏳

3min 15sec

Answers
on page 175

A | B | C | D | E

Best in Show

The results are in, and we have a winner. It's you!
(Assuming you found all the differences.)

12
changes

KEEP
SCORE

4min 30sec

Answers
on page 175

A

B

C

D

E

1   2   3   4   5

TOM KIDD/ALAMY

Can You Bear It?

Pay extra attention to this one, or things
could get grizzly

A
—
B
—
C
—
D
—
E

1 | 2 | 3 | 4 | 5

9
changes
- - - - - - - -
KEEP
SCORE

❏
❏
❏
❏
❏
❏
❏
❏
❏

4min 45sec

Answers
on page 175

One Big Fowl-up
Can you put these birds of a feather
back together?

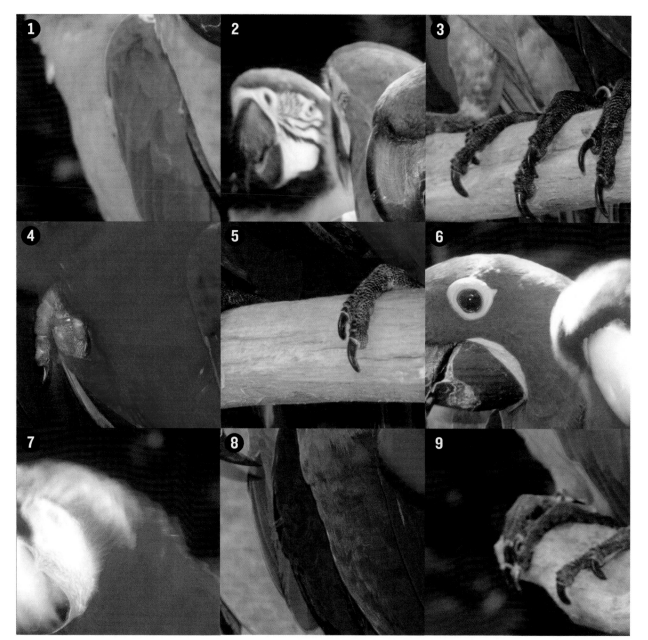

2min 45sec

Answer
on page 175

KEEP SCORE

Scrambled Eggs

This scene needs rearranging.
So hop to it.

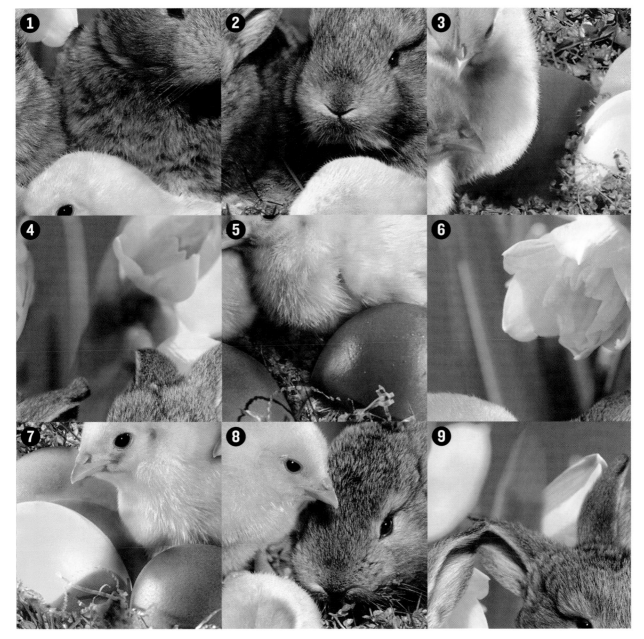

KEEP SCORE

3min 20sec

Answer
on page 175

Flying the Coop

Don't chicken out! Some feathery friends need your help
locating the updates to the farm.

10
changes

- - - - - - - -

KEEP
SCORE

A

—

B

—

C

—

D

—

E

⧗

3min 50sec

Answers
on page 175

1   2   3   4   5

Trunk Show

Check on the progress of the gentle giants
in the photos below

11
changes
- - - - - - - -
KEEP
SCORE

5min 5sec

Answers
on page 175

Home Stretch

You're almost done with this section. We *know* you can do it.

A | B | C | D | E

1 | 2 | 3 | 4 | 5

10
changes
- - - - - - - - -
KEEP
SCORE

❑ ❑ ❑ ❑ ❑ ❑ ❑ ❑ ❑ ❑

6min 10sec

Answers
on page 175

Stumped Yet?

Okay, we'll admit it: This one is going to bug you

5

4

3

2

1

A | B | C | D | E

10
changes
- - - - - - - - -
KEEP
SCORE

10min 50sec

Answers
on page 175

LIFE
CLASS

ICS [

These puzzles were
specially created with
memorable photos
from the LIFE archives.

]

Ground Control

Here's the scoop: You need to uncover 11 differences. Dig?

A

—

B

—

C

—

D

—

E

1 | 2 | 3 | 4 | 5

11
changes
- - - - - - - -
KEEP
SCORE

❑
❑
❑
❑
❑
❑
❑
❑
❑
❑
❑

⧗

7min 10sec

Answers
on page 175

Odds and Ends

Notice anything unusual?

A
—
B
—
C
—
D
—
E

1 | 2 | 3 | 4 | 5

11
changes

KEEP
SCORE
❑
❑
❑
❑
❑
❑
❑
❑
❑
❑
❑

⧖
6min 35sec

Answers
on page 176

Signs Are Good

Remember: They'll point you in the right direction

9
changes

- - - - - - - -

KEEP
SCORE

6min 10sec

Answers
on page 176

Go to Town

Who says there's nothing new on Main Street?

A

—

B

—

C

—

D

—

E

1 | 2 | 3 | 4 | 5

11
changes

- - - - - - - -

KEEP
SCORE

❏
❏
❏
❏
❏
❏
❏
❏
❏
❏
❏

⌛

7min 25sec

Answers
on page 176

They're Playing Our Song

These pictures are not *quite* in harmony

A
—
B
—
C
—
D
—
E

1   2   3   4   5

12
changes
- - - - - - - -
KEEP
SCORE

⏳
5min 30sec

Answers
on page 176

Construction Sight

Can you spot a whole pile of differences?

12
changes

KEEP
SCORE

A

–

B

–

C

–

D

–

E

6min 5sec

Answers
on page 176

1   2   3   4   5

Lawn and Order

There's a place for everything—and then some—under the sun

10
changes

KEEP
SCORE

❑ ❑ ❑ ❑ ❑ ❑ ❑ ❑ ❑ ❑

⧖
6min 55sec

Answers
on page 176

Stay on Track

You're almost at the finish line. And you're going to trot
right through this one, aren't you?

A

B

C

D

E

1   2   3   4   5

10
changes
- - - - - - - - -
KEEP
SCORE

❏
❏
❏
❏
❏
❏
❏
❏
❏
❏

⧗
7min 20sec

Answers
on page 176

Hammer Time

To frame it for you: There are 10 changes to find.
See how fast you can bang this out.

A
—
B
—
C
—
D
—
E

1 | 2 | 3 | 4 | 5

10
changes
- - - - - - - - -
KEEP
SCORE

❑
❑
❑
❑
❑
❑
❑
❑
❑
❑

⌛

7min 0sec

Answers
on page 176

Read Any Good Books Lately?

Other than this one, of course

15
changes
- - - - - - - -
KEEP
SCORE
❏ ❏ ❏ ❏ ❏ ❏ ❏ ❏ ❏ ❏ ❏ ❏ ❏ ❏ ❏

9min 20sec

Answers
on page 176

[ANSWERS]

Finished already? Let's see how you did.

[INTRODUCTION]

Page 3: Make a Splash No. 1 (A4): A window's been boarded up. No. 2 (B1): The garden has sunflowers. No. 3 (B2): Good thing Junior has protective eyewear. No. 4 (C3): Did you hear the news? He's been voted No. 1 Dad! No. 5 (C3 to C4): Bombs away! No. 6 (C5 to D5): Sis has come armed with reinforcements. No. 7 (D5 to E5): Thanks to extra watering, the grass has overgrown the sidewalk. No. 8 (E2 to E3): The lounge chair's support bar has straightened out. No. 9 (E4): She's slipped on her shoes.

[NOVICE]

Page 8: Farm Team No. 1 (A1 to A2): Is there a beaver around here, too? A tree has gone missing. No. 2 (B2): The door is now specially marked. No. 3 (B4): Which way is the wind blowing? No. 4 (C1): Happy Halloween! No. 5 (C2 to D2): Her necktie has been extended. Nos. 6, 7, and 8 (C4): Hey, Mary, we found your little lamb, but we seem to have lost a pumpkin. Meanwhile, here's a Rorschach test: Do you see a horse pattern on the cow's head? No. 9 (E2): Didn't Mom tell you not to go out in bear feet? No. 10 (E5): His shoe stripes now match the pumpkin.

Page 10: Made in the Shade No. 1 (B2): The green hat is now stylishly stripy. No. 2 (B3): Buy a hat, and he throws in the sunglasses for free. Nos. 3 and 4 (B4): A flower now decorates this brim. And is that chapeau seasick? It looks a little green. No. 5 (C1): Does headwear get sunburned? No. 6 (C1 to D1): More inventory has arrived. No. 7 (C3): That's not a brim—that's an awning. No. 8 (C5 to D5): Now *that's* a doggie bag. No. 9 (D2 to E2): Bottles have slipped to the right. No. 10 (E1 to E2): Look, a message in a bottle! (It says "Help, I can't stop doing these puzzles.") **Did you find the secret bonus difference?** If not, log on to *www.LIFE.com* to find out what it is.

Page 12: Getting Crafty No. 1 (B2 to C2): Let's make that a little less edgy. No. 2 (B4): The purple paper is longer. No. 3 (B4 to C3): Someone's been doodling. No. 4 (B5): Another green strip has been added to the mix. No. 5 (C1): A new purple page has appeared. No. 6 (C2 to C3): The pink shape has swiveled around. No. 7 (C4): Someone got sharp and closed the scissors. No. 8 (D2): Brian does good work. No. 9 (D3): Circle up, everyone.

Page 13: Hook, Line, and Sinker No. 1 (A1 to B1): The canister has done a 180. No. 2 (A2): The bobber's colors have switched sides. That'll fool those fish. No. 3 (A5): Another bobber's bobbed up. No. 4 (B2 to C2): Cracks you up, right? But then, you've always been a little nutty. No. 5 (B3 to B4): Whose lures are those? No. 6 (B3 to C3): A die was cast. No. 7 (B5 to C5): There are now two gold pieces. No. 8 (D4): Watch that wandering eye, buster. No. 9 (E1 to E2): Bye-bye, bobber.

Page 14: Double Vision No. 1 (A4 to B4): That's a major work of art. No. 2 (B1): Could someone lower the light, please? Thanks. No. 3 (B5): Tassels: nice touch. No. 4 (C1): That portrait totally flipped! No. 5 (C3): A little Visine would fix that red-eye. No. 6 (C3 to D3): Dude, what's in your pocket? No. 7 (D1 to D2): Two pillows? Nap time! Nos. 8 and 9 (D2): He's got the munchies. But who's got the buttons? No. 10 (D4 to D5): Looks like he hung up the ornaments. Somewhere. No. 11 (D5): The photo faded to black. No. 12 (E2 to E4): His jeans are now wide-legged.

Page 15: Simple Directions No. 1 (A2): Interurban has moved to the burbs. No. 2 (A4): The plane, Boss, the plane! No. 3 (B1 to C1): *Eek!* A spider! No. 4 (B3 to E3): Who painted the pole? No. 5 (B5): Expect a *loooong* journey to Louvre. No. 6 (C2 to C3): How will we ever get to Lenin now? No. 7 (D1 to D2): Xanadu and Canada always did have a lot in common. No. 8 (D5): Timbuktu just got a wee bit closer. No. 9 (E2): Foundry is heading south. No. 10 (E5): That window has a fancy new set of shutters.

Page 16: It's a Scorcher No. 1 (A1 to A2): The wall has reached for the sky. No. 2 (A3 to A4): Were those peppers hot *and* heavy? No. 3 (B5): That was one enlightened cow. It had a third eye. No. 4 (C2): That shadow seems incomplete somehow. No. 5 (C3 to D2): The wagon wheel has been detailed (by Prince's purple people, perhaps). No. 6 (C3 to D3): One spoke split. No. 7 (D1): That pepper's teetering on the edge. No. 8 (D4): Ever get the feeling you're being watched? No. 9 (E5): That wall's really got things pegged.

Page 18: Along Came a Spider No. 1 (A1 to A2): We're talking big picture here. No. 2 (A2 to B2): She put on a bracelet. No. 3 (A4 to C4): A strip of wallpaper has been stripped away. No. 4 (B1): The pendulum has swung the other way. No. 5 (C4 to D5): Little Miss Muffet has been disconnected. No. 6 (D1): Look, a mouse pad. No. 7 (D2 to D3): The chair got a third rung. No. 8 (E4): Hey, spidey—where you goin'?

Page 20: Petals Pushed No. 1 (A1 to A2): FLOWER POWER is this crafter's slogan. No. 2 (A5): This compartment has been emptied out. No. 3 (B1 to B2): A pink petal has infiltrated the gold ones. No. 4 (B5): That pink flower has really filled out. No. 5 (C2): Some petals are on the rise. No. 6 (C3): The flower's center is sunny yellow. No. 7 (D1 to D2): That petal is awfully pretty in pink. No. 8 (D1 to E1): The rosebud has rolled over. No. 9 (D4 to D5): No use crying over spilled paint. No. 10 (E2 to E3): There's plenty of orange paint to go around. Nos. 11 and 12 (E4 to E5): We've lost a paintbrush but gained some leaves.

Page 22: Extra! Extra! No. 1 (A4 to B4): The sky's the limit for that little blue box. No. 2 (B1): Nice new sticker. No. 3 (B2): The yellow label stands for quality. No. 4 (B3): The red bin is for short stories only. No. 5 (B4): And we now know that freedom is . . . a double blue line? No. 6 (B5): Wait, you forgot your soda! No. 7 (C1): Want to pick up some easy cash? No. 8 (C4 to C5): No parking! No. 9 (D4 to D5): The arrow is making a U-turn. No. 10 (E1 to E5): A broken yellow line means passing is permitted. Passing this test of your puzzle skills is also permitted.

Page 23: All Ears No. 1 (A1 to A2): Another cloud has floated in. No. 2 (A3): This tree's got some Christmas spirit. No. 3 (C1): Can you hear me now? No. 4 (C3): To avoid any confusion, the mailbox has been clearly labeled . . . in case the mailman dares to deliver! No. 5 (D1): Doggy's got a bone. No. 6 (D3 to E3): There's a new crack in the cement. No. 7 (D4): This pup's lost his ID tag. No. 8 (D5): She's wagged her tail right into view. No. 9 (E5): Beware, felines: No kitty trespassing allowed! **Did you find the secret bonus difference?** If not, log on to *www.LIFE.com* to find out what it is.

Page 24: Focus on the Present No. 1 (A2): Another gold ball was just what that tree needed. No. 2 (A4): The ribbon now drapes over both edges of the package. No. 3 (A5): This room just doesn't say Christmas yet; let's hang a wreath! No. 4 (A5 to B5): The poinsettia's been reappointed. No. 5 (B1): An ornament has ballooned. No. 6 (B4): One dot has dashed. No. 7 (C2): Looks like she needed an extra hand with that pile. No. 8 (C4): *X* marks the spot. No. 9 (D1 to E1): Now, *definitely* no one is opening that gift until Christmas. No. 10 (E3): How did she pull up her socks with her hands so full?

Page 26: I Do! Groom No. 3's boutonniere is blue instead of pink.

Page 27: If the Shoe Fits . . . No. 2 is the standout. The pair at top right is missing its logos.

Page 28: Hats? Sure. Hard? Nah. No. 1 (A1): Another wooden block has arrived. No. 2 (A1 to A5): Ouch, that board really got hammered. No. 3 (B4 to C5): This hat is reversible. No. 4 (C1 to C2): What the *helmet* is going on? No. 5 (C5): You're a star! No. 6 (D2 to E2): Someone's been collecting stickers. No. 7 (D3 to E4): Is Paul Bunyan working at this site? No. 8 (D4): Here's a hat that had more to say. No. 9 (D5): Jose? No way. No. 10 (E5): The foreman forgot his keys.

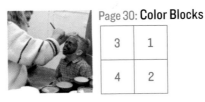

Page 30: Color Blocks

3	1
4	2

Page 31: This Does Not Compute

4	3
2	1

Page 32: What Up, Dawg? No. 1 (A3): No speeding. You're in a school zone now. No. 2 (A4 to A5): Someone removed the railing. No. 3 (B2): His patch has migrated. No. 4 (B4 to C5): You know that old saying about how owners and dogs look alike? No. 5 (C2): Hot dog! Almost like lunching at the ballpark. No. 6 (C3): Looks like we can't call him Patches anymore. No. 7 (C5): Beware of the saber-toothed dog! No. 8 (D1): The red apple has turned green. No. 9 (D1 to D2): The handle has come loose. No. 10 (D5): See, that's why his name is Spot. No. 11 (E2): Put him in, Coach, he's ready to play!

Page 34: Get Ready to Order No. 1 (A1): Sorry, those booths are no longer available. No. 2 (A3): Do you sit up straighter in high-backed chairs? No. 3 (A4): The artwork has tilted. No. 4 (B1): This seat boasts a new pattern. No. 5 (B5): Coffee, anyone? No. 6 (C2): Caution: wet floor. No. 7 (C2 to C4): The tabletop's gotten woodier. No. 8 (D5): That seat is extra-secure now. No. 9 (E1 to E2): The flooring's outline is now white. No. 10 (E3): The table is completely off base.

Page 35: Mug Shot No. 1 (A2 to B2): With two preservers, that mug is a real lifesaver. No. 2 (B1): There are no openings at the lighthouse. No. 3 (B4): Fido has a brand-new collar. No. 4 (D1 to E2): Perfect for a short cup of coffee. No. 5 (D2 to E3): The stripes have been fruitful and multiplied. No. 6 (D3 to E3): This blossom is blossoming. Nos. 7 and 8 (D4): Hey, ya mug, thought you could pull a fast one? Well, we have your prints. Meanwhile, that other flower's been retouched. No. 9 (D5 to E5): Can you get a handle on this? No. 10 (E4): Someone spilled in the cupboard. What a mess! **Did you find the secret bonus difference?** If not, log on to *www.LIFE.com* to find out what it is.

Page 36: Tiptoe Through the Treetops No. 1 (A2 to A3): Two more windows adorn the pink hideaway. No. 2 (B1): Part of the railing has been boarded up. No. 3 (B2): No, seriously, KEEP OUT! No. 4 (B3): The kid has crossed the bridge. Nos. 5 and 6 (C3): The window in the door is no more, while the window above it all is now small. No. 7 (C3 to C4): More birds have flown in to check out the construction. No. 8 (C5): This bucket's been supersized. No. 9 (D1): Okay, who cut down the trees? No. 10 (D1 to E1): More wood has been added to the pile. No. 11 (E3): A new crew has joined the painting party.

Page 37: Can You Dig It? No. 1 (A1): Another flower's bloomed on the wall. No. 2 (A2 to B2): That window is feeling a little less pane. No. 3 (A3 to A4): Two plus two equals four. No. 4 (B2 to B3): One shovel head has gotten bigger. No. 5 (C1): The shovel has swiveled. No. 6 (C5): The Man in the Moon is all smiles. No. 7 (D2): That handle sure has grown. No. 8 (D5): Rusted wall hangings: banned. No. 9 (E1): The extra patch of siding is gone. No. 10 (E4): One piece has moved to a new spot.

Page 38: It's a Grand Old Flag No. 1 (A1): A flag has paraded out of the picture. No. 2 (A1 to B1): That flag will wave a lot longer now. No. 3 (A4): Apparently some states have seceded. No. 4 (A5 to B5): Another blue column's been added. No. 5 (B4): That's one pumped-up pinwheel. No. 6 (C1 to D1): The stripes are now vertical. No. 7 (C2 to C3): Now *she's* star-spangled. No. 8 (C4 to C5): Her straps are well-tied. No. 9 (D1 to E2): Red ruffles are all the rage. No. 10 (E5): Her stars have faded.

Page 40: Game, Set, Match No. 1 (B2): She's a star! According to her shoulder, anyway. No. 2 (B3): Score: two balls to none. No. 3 (B5): The court has been extended. No. 4 (C3): Wristband from the Rainbow Brite Collection. Nos. 5 and 6 (C4): Oh, you're right: Pearls are so classy, especially with a simpler top. No. 7 (C5): A line was crossed (out). No. 8 (D1): In other fashion news, longer shorts are in. No. 9 (E5): The red dot shifted over.

Page 42: Of Mice and Man No. 1 (A1 to A3): Why, that window looks like it expects a hanging. No. 2 (A4 to A5): Nice paint job. No. 3 (B2): The window has been relieved of a pane. No. 4 (B3): Well, well, aren't you just Mr. Microphone. Nos. 5 and 6 (B5): The photo's been reframed (and quite nicely, too). And it looks like real men *do* get pedicures. Nos. 7 and 8 (C2): Miss Mouse has appeared in the window. Plus a few more buttons have been sewn on his shirt. No. 9 (C3 to D4): That fireplace is a few bricks shy. Nos. 10 and 11 (C5): The lampshade is leaning at a new angle, while the chair's back is more ornate. No. 12 (D1): His legs got longer. No. 13 (D1 to E1): There's a new purple line on the blanket. No. 14 (D2): She's changed her shoes. No. 15 (D3 to D4): Fire! No. 16 (D4): She looks familiar. No. 17 (D5 to E5): There are only two drawers now. Nos. 18 and 19 (E2): One chair leg has been extended—definitely a step forward. And he left his headphones on the floor. No. 20 (E5): Welcome to tinsel town!

[MASTER]

Page 46: Key Quest Nos. 1 and 2 (A2): It's easy to turn yellow when the heart is involved. Meanwhile, two more holes have been drilled into that button. No. 3 (A3 to B2): The purple diamond grew up, then swapped places with the blue diamond. What would Lucky Charms make of that? No. 4 (A4): The button's green center has been downsized. No. 5 (B2 to C2): The red button has rotated. No. 6 (B4 to C4): The yin-and-yang symbol has lost its dots. No. 7 (B5): That mother-of-pearl one won't be sewn up anytime soon. No. 8 (C2): A rose-shaped button's been repeated. No. 9 (C3): The etchings on the key have been erased. No. 10 (C5): The brooch decided not to make a cameo appearance. No. 11 (E2): There's another bead. No. 12 (E4): Someone swiped the stone!

Page 48: It's in the Bag No. 1 (A1): This bag's got a brand-new tag. No. 2 (A4 to A5): Look, Ma! No handles! No. 3 (B2): The pink stripes have been connected. No. 4 (B3): The bag's been cornered. In no time, the leather will have it surrounded! No. 5 (B4): That red bag is really deep, man. No. 6 (B5): This purse is all about the label. No. 7 (D1 to E1): The yellow and the white have swapped sides. No. 8 (D4 to E3): There's more purple on this purse. No. 9 (E2 to E3): The bag's corners have stopped hanging around. **Did you find the secret bonus difference?** If not, log on to *www.LIFE.com* to find out what it is.

Page 49: Tidying Up No. 1 (A3 to B3): Time weighs heavily on this kitchen. No. 2 (A4 to A5): The cabinets should be twice as easy to open. No. 3 (B1): Grandma, is that you? No. 4 (B2 to C2): Dig that space-age TV set. No. 5 (B5): Two owls—what a hoot! No. 6 (C1): There's been an increase in cookware, too. No. 7 (C3 to D4): Wondermom opted for the utility-belt look today. No. 8 (D2): One knob has drifted a bit. No. 9 (D3 to E2): Who unplugged the TV? No. 10 (E1 to E2): That extra storage will come in handy.

Page 50: Off-Kilter Nos. 1 and 2 (A1): The position of the chain *chain-chain-changed*. And when do you think he tees off? No. 3 (A2): He lost his pinkie ring. No. 4 (A3): He's more buckled up than before. No. 5 (A5): Would you say that new triangle of buttons on his pocket is equilateral or isosceles? No. 6 (B2): He lost a stripe from his jacket. No. 7 (B4): More tape's been added to the pole. No. 8 (C4 to C5): He's sporting a new pouch. No. 9 (D3): There's something about a man with a big tassel. No. 10 (D4 to D5): Stripes really suit these guys. No. 11 (E3): Let's face it: There's just no such thing as too many sock ribbons. No. 12 (E5): Don't know if he has two left feet, but he's definitely wearing two left socks.

Page 51: Rain Delay No. 1 (A1 to A5): The awning is now on the straight and narrow. No. 2 (A2): Two more clothespins have hopped on line. No. 3 (B1 to C2): The towel's stripes have switched colors. No. 4 (B4): Those shorts must be made of stretch fabric. Nos. 5 and 6 (C1): The reflector has replicated, while the hubcap's looking less porous. No. 7 (C2): Cover your belly, young lady. Nos. 8 and 9 (C4): And you shield those shoulders, buddy. But we see you've added a stripe to your inflatable. Nice work. No. 10 (C4 to C5): My, that's a big bike seat. No. 11 (C5): A handlebar took a sharp turn upward. No. 12 (D1): The cooler did a 180. No. 13 (D3): Mom's kicked off her shoes to enjoy the . . . rain?

Page 52: Chilly Dogs No. 1 (A4): A hinge sledded southward. No. 2 (B3): That pooch has reversed his purples. No. 3 (B3 to D4): The sleigh's front panel has lost its gold trim. No. 4 (B4): That's one big bell. No. 5 (C1 to C2): It must be a warm winter—Santa took off his hat. No. 6 (C2): Don't trip on that scarf, doggy. No. 7 (C3): The sled's decorative snowflake has snowballed. No. 8 (D1): Santa's packing his sack and tying it twice. No. 9 (D4 to D5): Want to play fetch? No. 10 (D5): That extra bolt should deter break-ins. No. 11 (E5): Hey, Goldie—you lost a stripe.

Page 54: Pretty in Pink No. 1 (A3): Violets must be out of season. No. 2 (A4): That bowl has gotten leafier. No. 3 (A4 to B4): There's a new cake in town. No. 4 (A5 to B5): How polite—someone has cleared those plates. Nos. 5 and 6 (B2): Who ordered the hot chocolate with marshmallows? And a shorter spoon? No. 7 (D2): That fork's less ornate but still works great. No. 8 (D3 to D4): That's a mighty big blossom. No. 9 (D5): One cupcake picked up more pink dots. No. 10 (E1): A metallic ball took a fall.

Page 55: Rake It In No. 1 (A1 to A2): *X* marks the spot. No. 2 (A4): Four new bricks have been laid. No. 3 (A5): Darn these graffiti artists! No. 4 (B3): One rake turned over a new leaf. No. 5 (C1): *Another* garbage receptacle?

How trashy. No. 6 (C2): One garden implement is looking a bit more orangey. No. 7 (C3): That rake's price hasn't fallen, but it *has* rotated. No. 8 (C4 to E4): Someone's handle has been painted blue. No. 9 (D1 to E1): The white lid's been spun round—like a record, baby. No. 10 (D2): That tool's head has been made longer. No. 11 (D5 to E5): Is he nuts? This is no place for a squirrel!

Page 56: Liquid Assets No. 1 (A1): Someone bought a bottle. No. 2 (A2 to B2): Did that guy switch hats? No. 3 (A4): The handle has plumped up. No. 4 (A5 to B5): The blue cap is taller. No. 5 (B3): The orange tag has slipped off to the side. No. 6 (C1 to D2): The red cap has undergone a redesign (down to its tag). No. 7 (D2): The tag has swelled. Hope the price hasn't. No. 8 (D3): This cap is showing off its stripes. No. 9 (D4): A dollar sign's been drawn in. No. 10 (D5): $2.16: bargain. $2.19: outrage. No. 11 (E5): The product label has inched up the bottle.

Page 57: 'Tis the Season . . . Nos. 1 and 2 (A2): One snowman has an extra ball on his hat, while the other has a brand-new button. No. 3 (B1): Mr. Snowman seems to have changed his perspective. No. 4 (B2): Yep, two scarves are better than one. No. 5 (B4): Something has made Mrs. Claus very happy. No. 6 (B5): Who lost a hat? No. 7 (C1): Santa outgrew his belt. But then, you know, no one likes a skinny Santa. No. 8 (C3): Love the red-and-white topper. No. 9 (D5): She's sporting a longer skirt. No. 10 (E2): The angel's doubled up on her drums. No. 11 (E5): More presents!

Page 58: Another Bloomin' Puzzle No. 1 (A1): Another leaf has grown. No. 2 (A2 to B2): That pole has grown, too. No. 3 (B3 to C4): Sweet stripes, Grandpa! No. 4 (B4): That brown stone got huge. No. 5 (C1 to D1): The round stonework sure has stacked up. No. 6 (C2): The shell has turned over. No. 7 (C2 to C3): *Two* gnomes? Too much! No. 8 (C4): The number of mushrooms has, uh, mushroomed. No. 9 (C4 to D4): Did that hand's fingers do the walking? No. 10 (C4 to E4): Gramps dropped a few stripes, too. No. 11 (C5): A little pink bloom took off. No. 12 (D1 to E1): The garden's now all ramped up. No. 13 (E2): Some flowers just grow like weeds. No. 14 (E4): Looks like he needs a trowel rack.

Page 59: Housing Crunch No. 1 (A4 to C5): A skywriter's flown by. No. 2 (B1): Just when you think you know everything about the top story, there's more to it. No. 3 (B3): A new chimney's been installed. No. 4 (C3): A window's been bricked over. No. 5 (C5): Someone must be completely receptive, given that antenna. No. 6 (D1): Another window was put in. No. 7 (D4): That's a room with an askew view. Nos. 8 and 9 (E3): The tiny window tiptoed over, while the house next door drilled down. No. 10 (E5): Gone with the window?

Page 60: Honk if You Spot It No. 2 is up to no good. The red car in the bottom row is smuggling an extra pink package.

Page 61: Patio Daddy-O Not to harsh your mellow, but No. 5 is out of marshmallows.

Page 62: Quantum Leap No. 1 (A1 to A2): The bookcase is looking increasingly shelf-ish. No. 2 (A3 to A4): The green fabric is wrinkle-free. No. 3 (B2): Does bottled water flow north? No. 4 (B3): She didn't need that purple undershirt, anyway. No. 5 (B5): Her watch appears to be elbow-bound. No. 6 (C1 to C2): The 4 has been carried over. No. 7 (C4): Chalk reinforcements have arrived. No. 8 (D1 to E3): Cupid's arrow bags another victim. No. 9 (D2): We'll give that new number a 10 on the wackiness scale. No. 10 (D4): *Aww,* there's a whole lotta love here.

Page 64: Bumper Crop No. 1 (A1): The pattern on the tarp is looking less see-through. No. 2 (A2): She has slipped off her scrunchies. No. 3 (B1 to B2): Talk about a sugar rush! No. 4 (B3): His overalls strap is anchored deeper. No. 5 (B5): His shirt seems to be going gray. No. 6 (D1): Her ankle was feeling modest. No. 7 (D3 to E3): The railing needed some extra support. No. 8 (D4): An insignia got bumped off the bumper car. No. 9 (D4 to D5): Matching shoes are so overrated. No. 10 (D5): One car upgraded its taillight. No. 11 (E1): Better double-wrap that cord.

Page 66: Are You Ready to Rock? No. 1 (B1): The carrot careened off-course. Nos. 2 and 3 (B2): The cutting board's been cut down to size. But that carrot sure is flourishing. No. 4 (B5): You can grip that colander twice as easily now. Nos. 5 and 6 (C1): A cheeseburger? Well done! Meanwhile, one knob has dropped. Nos. 7 and 8 (C4 to C5): Anyone who plays a spatula must have flipped. And apparently the recipe called for a *large* saucepan. No. 9 (C5): The white bowl's been whitewashed. No. 10 (E2): Yeah, he doesn't seem like the kind of guy who needs matching laces. No. 11 (E5): Someone's been messing with the tile floor.

Page 68: Inner Peace No. 1 (A4): The stack of mats is taller. No. 2 (A5): The wooden decoration has rotated. No. 3 (B1): This snout has been stretched. No. 4 (B4 to C4): The poster's center has expanded (much like this lady's consciousness). No. 5 (C2): Another flowerpot now sits on the windowsill. No. 6 (C5 to D5): A pillow has plumped up. No. 7 (D3): The outlet has relocated. Nos. 8 and 9 (D4): She may not need her watch to meditate, but she is now ready to write down anything that pops to mind. No. 10 (E1): One of the pillow's characters has moved. **Did you find the secret bonus difference? If not, log on to** *www.LIFE.com* **to find out what it is.**

Page 69: Quit Clowning Around No. 1 (A3): Bozo's got a balloon. No. 2 (B1 to B2): The fire truck lost a stripe. No. 3 (B2): Looks like some firemen have been clowning around, too. No. 4 (B4): Hate to put you on the spot, clownie, but what's up with your hat? No. 5 (B4 to C4): Someone's schnoz is looking a bit more . . . bulbous. No. 6 (C5): Guess this is a one-lane road now. No. 7 (D3): The jester on the car wigged out (and opted for purple). No. 8 (E1): The googly eyes have gone haywire. No. 9 (E3): One star has lost a point. No. 10 (E4): What a lot of dots. No. 11 (E5): The wheel must be blushing.

Page 70: Think Outside the Lines No. 1 (A5 to B5): Looks like someone bought the red painting. No. 2 (B1 to D1): Can you really erase paint like that? No. 3 (B3 to C3): Squeeze his sweater and more yarn comes out. No. 4 (B4 to C5): Her locks are now longer. No. 5 (D2 to E2): You can't spell "masterpiece" without an *A*. No. 6 (D3): The "tube" has been relabeled. No. 7 (D4): His cuff is now blue. No. 8 (E1): Be careful reaching for those crayons. No. 9 (E4 to E5): Can't have too many brushes.

Page 72: Bedroom Brainteaser No. 1 (A3 to A4): That mattress is twice as nice. Nos. 2 and 3 (B1): Are those Russian nesting dolls replicating? And another tiny picture has been hung. No. 4 (B3): The red box has shrunk. No. 5 (B3 to C3): More windows have joined the door. No. 6 (B4): All of the borders in the right column are now yellow. No. 7 (C2): Kitty gets around. No. 8 (C5): Where'd that support bar go? No. 9 (D1): The bottle's looking tipsy. No. 10 (D2 to D3): You never know when a microphone will sneak up on you. No. 11 (E4): Both of the ladder's feet now extend out of the frame.

Page 73: Wash and Go No. 1 (A2): Let's just say this change is all about eaves. No. 2 (A4 to A5): The blinds have been closed; maybe Mom is trying to sleep. No. 3 (C1): What's up with that door handle? No. 4 (C3): That hairdo is so avant-garde. Nos. 5 and 6 (C5): The garage door design got smaller, and the sticker moved up. No. 7 (D2): The hubcap holes have been filled in. No. 8 (D4): He's changed his stripes. No. 9 (E1 to E2): The puddle is growing.

Page 74: Everything Must Go

6	4
1	5
2	3

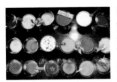

Page 75: Snail Mail

4	3
5	1
6	2

Page 76: Bowled Over No. 1 (A3): The center of this flower has wilted. No. 2 (A3 to A4): Someone's been rearranging the display again. No. 3 (A5): Hey, Mr. Ceramic Pot—you're missing a spot (up top)! No. 4 (B1 to C2): The blue bloom went *boom*. No. 5 (B5): And this pot's pattern lines now intersect. No. 6 (C1 to D5): A little yellow paint really perks up the table rim. No. 7 (C4): Find a quarter, pick it up—find three more, you've got a buck. No. 8 (D5): Is that a genuine crushed-red-velvet interior? No. 9 (E2): Hello, new flower. No. 10 (E4): One more leaf couldn't hurt.

Page 78: Meow Mix-ups No. 1 (A1): Knock, knock. *Who's there?* Orange. *Orange who?* Orange you glad this chair isn't in your dining room? No. 2 (A3): Kitty's picked a flower. No. 3 (A4): A blue cushion tuft is now purple. No. 4 (B2 to B3): Violet blooms have sprouted. No. 5 (B5 to C5): This garden's due for a sprinkle. No. 6 (C1 to D1): Just dump that new soil right next to the sofa, fellas. No. 7 (C3 to D3): Kitty's tail has grown. No. 8 (C5 to D5): The planter's proportions have shifted. No. 9 (D2 to D3): The slipcover had some slippage. No. 10 (E3 to E4): The yellow stone under the couch has inched forward.

Page 79: The Bar Is Raised No. 1 (A2): Don't you love a crazy straw? No. 2 (A3 to A4): The toffee on top has tilted. No. 3 (A4 to A5): This drink is totally nutty. No. 4 (B5 to C5): Picky, picky. No. 5 (C1 to C2): Two drinks have traded places. No. 6 (C4): Berry nice garnish. No. 7 (D2): The sticker turned green. No. 8 (D4): Confidential to mint sprig: We especially leaf you. No. 9 (E3): Apparently, flowers thrive in tomato juice. No. 10 (E5): When life hands you lemons, float one in your drink.

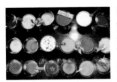

Page 80: Hunting Party No. 1 (A1): Trees mature quickly here in, um, France. No. 2 (A2): There's a new window. No. 3 (A3): Things just got a little more arch. No. 4 (A5): It's curtains for this window. No. 5 (B1): Hey—those

baskets bailed. No. 6 (B4): Wait, wait, don't tell us: Fu Manchu, right? No. 7 (B5): Now where did we put that window? No. 8 (C1): We've decided to take a different path. No. 9 (C2 to D2): Dude, whatever that stuff is on your chest, it's multiplying. Nos. 10 and 11 (C3): Flouting the current fashion for plunging necklines, she's raised hers, then pinned on a brooch for good measure. No. 12 (C5): Someone forget a basket? No. 13 (D2 to E2): If only that actually fit like a glove. No. 14 (D3 to D4): An apple a day keeps the doctor away. Well, that and a prudent neckline. No. 15 (D5 to E5): That string has stretched.

[EXPERT]

Page 84: Market Madness No. 1 (A1): Purple and blue have flipped on this umbrella. No. 2 (A2): Madam, is that a hat or a lampshade? No. 3 (A3): A man has fled the scene. No. 4 (B2): She swapped her slippers. No. 5 (B4): The motorcyclist has added purchases. No. 6 (C1): The fruit has been fruitful. No. 7 (C3): She's tugged her sleeve down her wrist. No. 8 (D3): Don't buy that egg, lady—it's a lemon. No. 9 (E2): Tell you what—we'll toss in an extra melon for free. No. 10 (E4): One papaya has unripened.

Page 86: Gettin' Wiggy With It No. 1 (A2 to A3): What lovely green eyes you have. No. 2 (A5): Her neck has lost its price tag. No. 3 (B1): That base is loaded—looks like it's doubled, in fact. No. 4 (B3): She's switched to Ray-Bans. No. 5 (C1): This wig's been restyled. No. 6 (C2 to C3): Lady—lay off the lip plumper. No. 7 (C4): Who got her bangs snipped? No. 8 (D1): The metal grid is gone. No. 9 (D2): Hey, move over. No. 10 (E2): Her tag turned 90 degrees. No. 11 (E3): There's a little girl with a wayward curl. No. 12 (E4): Love your new lipstick.

Page 87: Notes From a Marriage No. 1 (A2): The king no longer has a castle. No. 2 (A5): Parrot's loose again. Nos. 3 and 4 (B4): More flute to toot! And that collage has crept up the wall. No. 5 (B5): A block on the drape has been blocked out. No. 6 (C2): Is that an eggcup? No. 7 (D3): Hey, you kids, who's been carving up the furniture? Nos. 8 and 9 (D4): The red thread on Mom's shirt is longer. And Junior's reading big books now. No. 10 (E2): The trivet has traveled.

Page 88: Don't Lose Your Marbles No. 1 (A4 to A5): The orange line has thickened. No. 2 (B1): An orange guy has rotated. No. 3 (B2): A blue spot is on the move. No. 4 (C3 to D3): Someone's looking more speckled. Nos. 5 and 6 (C4): Dig that double stripe. And did you notice that the dark-green guy that was lurking in the background is now gone? Nos. 7 and 8 (C5): There's been a last-minute substitution: green for orange. And one white marble's been wiped clean. No. 9 (D3): The notch in that little blue one has grown into an equator. No. 10 (E1 to E2): A multihued marble is feeling bluer by the minute. **Did you find the secret bonus difference? If not, log on to *www.LIFE.com* to find out what it is.**

Page 90: **Island Breeze** No. 1 (A1): The tapestry is down one dot. No. 2 (B1): One petal has grown. No. 3 (B4): His shoulder has a sunnier disposition. No. 4 (B5): Time to restock the earrings. No. 5 (C1): The fringe is, well, fringier. No. 6 (C4): One child-sized hairpin, please. No. 7 (C5): Two stones have swapped spots. Nos. 8 and 9 (D1): An additional shell is shoring up one necklace, while another chain is missing some links. No. 10 (D3): The green necklace snuggled up to its neighbor. No. 11 (D5): That hole certainly has shrunk.

Page 92: **Over the Limit** No. 1 (A2): A red stripe now pulls up short. No. 2 (A3): The yellow label has lost its blue spot. Maybe it got stuck in customs. No. 3 (A4): That bag's lock has been picked—picked right off. No. 4 (B3): The guitar case now has—count 'em—three bottom rivets. No. 5 (B3 to B4): This trunk's been scratch-proofed. No. 6 (C3): The little gold plate has turned 90 degrees. No. 7 (C5): A clasp on the brown bag has lurched leftward. No. 8 (D2): Part of the latch has moved down. No. 9 (D5): The big brown trunk is triple-secure. No. 10 (E2): The red case earned a promotion. It now has three stripes. No. 11 (E3): The green suitcase lost one of its feet. Darn baggage handlers.

Page 94: **Distinctive Blend** The red canister just above the cash register in No. 5 doesn't stack up to the rest. Its leaf decoration has flipped.

Page 95: **Arcade Fun** No. 2 has seen a lane change. The dark strip on the second red bumper at left is shorter than the rest.

Page 96: **Grill, Interrupted** Nos. 1 and 2 (A4): Upon reflection, the branch chose not to use that window as a mirror. As for you, Dad, a midlife crisis is fine, but an *earring*? No. 3 (A5): Get Bob Vila on the blower—one of the eaves has dropped off. No. 4 (B1): That is one big bush. No. 5 (B3): The windowpane divider moved over. No. 6 (C2): Grandma's secret lemonade calls for a garnish of kiwifruit. No. 7 (D2): Would you look at that—a slat-less spatula. No. 8 (D5): With that superlong handle, Dad should get a good grip on the weenies. No. 9 (E2): Who ordered the jumbo burger? No. 10 (E3): A frank is looking less charred. No. 11 (E4): One dog learned to roll over.

Page 98: **Agony of the Feet** No. 1 (A3): A red tag sailed rightward. No. 2 (A4): New inventory arriving daily! No. 3 (A5): A box's hole has sunk. No. 4 (B1): This shoe is for the especially well-heeled. No. 5 (B2): Her shirt is extra-ornate now. No. 6 (B4 to C4): Another row of holes has been drilled into the shelving unit. No. 7 (C2): She donned another bracelet. Nos. 8 and 9 (C4): The price tag on the thongs has vanished. Maybe they're free now. Over to the right, that red sandal is feeling particularly strapped. No. 10 (D4): The purple fish on the strap has been scaled. No. 11 (E1 to E2): Her pants now cover her beautiful blue anklet. **Did you find the secret bonus difference? If not, log on to www.LIFE.com to find out what it is.**

Page 99: **Autumn Serenade** No. 1 (B3): No flag holder? Not very patriotic. Nos. 2 and 3 (B4): The pole has vaulted skyward, and the post has a double scoop of green. No. 4 (C2): Mr. Bear, the "walk like an Egyptian" gag is so 1986. No. 5 (C3): The mail slot's moved up. No. 6 (C5): The owl's head tilts the other way. No. 7 (D2): One arm has extra support. Nos. 8 and 9 (D3): A pumpkin that size could squash a man. And the scarecrow ain't talkin'. Nos. 10 and 11 (E4): Another sunflower has sprouted. And one hydrant screw is loose. Actually, it's on the loose.

Page 100: **Show of Hands** No. 1 (A3): A dot's darted down her ring finger. No. 2 (B1): A bloom now has a sparkly center. No. 3 (B4): A gold leaf has blown away. No. 4 (B4 to B5): A green gem for a pink one? Fair trade. No. 5 (C2): Some gold design in the shadow has disappeared. No. 6 (C3): One pink stone has grown more valuable. No. 7 (C4): A curlicue has twisted its torso. No. 8 (C5): The teardrop on her fingertip has extended. How sad. Nos. 9 and 10 (D1): You know, that extra bracelet really completes her outfit. And note that the petal at six o'clock is farther from the flower's center. No. 11 (D3): Better hurry—the line on her thumb is getting longer. No. 12 (D4): Her middle finger's tip has picked up a petal.

Page 102: **Read the Signs** No. 1 (B3): M.P.H. has been overly punctuated. No. 2 (B4): Oh, Mr. Hyphen, didn't you know beer can make you fat? No. 3 (B5): The 7's UP has actually moved down. No. 4 (C1): MÜNCHEN has steered to the left. Nos. 5 and 6 (C3): The rock has rolled away, and the husky's tail now curls downward. No. 7 (C5): The A stands out in a crowd: It's solid black now. No. 8 (D1): The Union Pacific sign has gotten rusty. Okay, *rustier*. No. 9 (D2): The H and the S have traded places. No. 10 (D3): The sun medallion has spun upside down. No. 11 (D4): The price tag has rotated 90 degrees.

Page 104: **All Tangoed Up**

2	9	7
11	10	5
12	6	1
4	3	8

Page 105: Window of Opportunity

8	3	4
6	10	12
11	1	7
2	9	5

Page 106: Boning Up No. 1 (A4): Careful—one plate has become quite pointy. No. 2 (B4): The dino in the wall display must have torn his ACL—his rearmost leg bones have been fused together. No. 3 (B5): Which may be why he's looking down. No. 4 (C2): The wall is a bit less square. Nos. 5 and 6 (C3): One rib has lengthened. And the tree in back sprouted a new leaf. No. 7 (C5 to D5): The white box has grown longer. No. 8 (D1 to D2): The display lettering is now single-spaced. No. 9 (D3): Sideburns are so prehistoric (circa 1998). No wonder he shaved his off. No. 10 (D5): A bone on the wall has flipped. No. 11 (E2): A hole's been filled in. No. 12 (E5): The slanted shadow at the right is wider.

Page 107: Surfin' Safari No. 1 (B1): One guy must have come ashore. Nos. 2 and 3 (B4): More duct tape has been affixed to this board's tip, and one wader has drifted left. Watch that undertow, buddy! No. 4 (C1): Both sides of the boogie board are now outlined. Nos. 5 and 6 (C2): A curved white line's been chopped into dashes, and her surfboard's squiggle has been stretched. Nos. 7 and 8 (C4): The tiny surfer icon has moved his arms. Plus, someone took the hyphen out of "C-25." That's a plus. No. 9 (C4 to D4): The board's white stripe now extends to the edges. No. 10 (C5): White line's been doubled. Nos. 11 and 12 (D1): Someone has picked up the litter. And that boat's going nowhere now. No. 13 (D3): One fin's been nixed. Hope the surfer can still steer!

Page 108: Playing Hardball No. 1 (A3): Picture this: Babe Ruth at bat. No. 2 (B1): The baseball-card box is now a bubble-gum box. No. 3 (B2): The wood paneling has been removed. No. 4 (B3): Ball three! No. 5 (B4): Are you calling Brooklyn yellow? No. 6 (B5 to C5): A pinstripe's been stripped. No. 7 (C4): One desk pigeonhole has been cleaned out. Nos. 8 and 9 (D1): Turns out the ball didn't need stitches. And that pinball machine sure is bolted down. No. 10 (D2): Need an extra bat? No. 11 (D3): The large *N* on the magazine has morphed into an *M*. No. 12 (E3): The number 72 is now 27. No. 13 (E4): That pitch on the cover of *Sport* magazine is out of sight!

Page 110: Ring-a-Ding-Ding! No. 1 (A1): Seeing spots? You should be. No. 2 (A2): The white *A* on the red ring is fatter. No. 3 (A4): The red circle at the center of the ring up top has been filled in with black. No. 4 (A4 to A5): The one with two yellow dots has been spared its

glare. No. 5 (B1): The blue arch (beneath the white *A*) has been fully filled in. No. 6 (B2 to B3): The fraternal twins have swapped places. No. 7 (B3 to C3): The concentric circles have a new color pattern. Nos. 8 and 9 (B5): The tide is rising on the orange ring, while on the pink ring, a brown dot has moved over. No. 10 (C3): An extra black triangle has squeezed in. No. 11 (D1): The swirl is swirlier. Nos. 12 and 13 (D2): Apparently it's cherry season. And a blue flower has grown over a white one. No. 14 (D3): Another white line has appeared on the one with hearts. No. 15 (D4): That blue stripe's looking a little chubby. No. 16 (D5): A second squiggle now brackets the design. No. 17 (E1): A pink dot has descended. No. 18 (E2): The bull's-eye has shifted its aim to the left. No. 19 (E3): Another black spoke has poked out of the flower on the left. No. 20 (E5): The black splotch's lower appendage is thicker.

[GENIUS]

Page 114: All Dolled Up No. 1 (A2 to B2): That fourth doll in the top row totally ripped off the apron of the doll below her. No. 2 (A3): An extra yellow pom-pom—kicky! Nos. 3 and 4 (A4): Someone lose her earrings? And we see the lady in red and blue has opted for more international headwear. No. 5 (B1): A skirt's black stripe has doubled in thickness. No. 6 (B4): Who'd have thought her red headdress could get *even more fabulous*! No. 7 (B4 to C4): Her shift picked up a stripe. No. 8 (C2): One blue flower blew away. No. 9 (C5): The sash now has double the green doodads. No. 10 (D2): Two dolls pulled a switcheroo! No. 11 (D3): Her ankle-length ponytail is now pigtails. (Is that you, Crystal Gayle?) No. 12 (D4): Holy beanstalk, Batman! She's growing! No. 13 (D5): Her apron has shrunk. No. 14 (E2 to E3): Someone did an abrupt about-face. No. 15 (E4): Her apron flower has flourished.

Page 116: Not to Scale No. 1 (A2): The red flipper's been flopped. No. 2 (A4): That tool looks a little sawed-off. No. 3 (B2): One wooden handle towers over the rest. Nos. 4 and 5 (B5): That tool has a new tilt. But the scissors have skedaddled. Nos. 6 and 7 (C2): The label seems to be creeping up. And that round guy has been reunited with its twin. Don't you love a happy ending? No. 8 (C4): An extra-large wrench might come in handy. No. 9 (D1): This model vehicle is sporting a new stripe. No. 10 (D4): His overalls button has gained in overall size. No. 11 (D5): The tape measure has more markings.

Page 118: Shuffled Cards No. 1 (A4): The design curves down now. No. 2 (B1): Another branch has grown into the winter scene. No. 3 (B4): The light's been turned off in one window (in anticipation of Santa's arrival, probably). No. 4 (C1): One exclamation mark slipped. No. 5 (C5): Someone really trimmed that tree on the white card. It's tiny now. No. 6 (D2): The snowman's hat has a jaunty new angle. Nos. 7 and 8 (D4): Sorry, doggies (and werewolves), the full moon has passed. Next door, the Christmas tree has positively flipped. No. 9 (E2): One white line has left this stock. No. 10 (E4): The North Star appears to be spinning. No. 11 (E5): One poinsettia leaf has been plucked.

Page 119: City Slickers No. 1 (A3): Sloppy, sloppy—his poncho now has two creases. No. 2 (B1): The yellow slicker's visor now has a black rim. Maybe it's tinted. Nos. 3 and 4 (B2): You in the red: Don't be shy. (It seems to be catching—the girl in green is showing less leg.) No. 5 (B4): His blue slicker's looking less green. No. 6 (B5): A yellow Conehead? Nos. 7 and 8 (C3): Her yellow jacket's been stung with a second design. And his cap's bill must have come due. No. 9 (C4): Is that a *handlebar* mustache? No. 10 (C5): Ms. Pointyhead's skirt lost a flower. No. 11 (D3): These pants have grown longer. No. 12 (E2): A red rear fender has been resized, downward. **Did you find the secret bonus difference?** If not, log on to *www.LIFE.com* to find out what it is.

Page 120: Lily Monster No. 1 (A5): One vertical strip of wood has dropped from the latticework. No. 2 (B1): A butterfly fluttered by. No. 3 (B2): Who plucked the white flowers? No. 4 (B3): A cluster of lilies has thickened. No. 5 (B5): One leaf has fallen from this tree. No. 6 (C3): More grass has shot up. No. 7 (C4): A trio of lily pads has floated to the left. No. 8 (C5): A red carnation has grown skyward. No. 9 (D2): Who's been clipping blooms? No. 10 (E1): Hello, new Mr. Yellow Flower. No. 11 (E5): One guy's been dyed purple.

Page 122: Broken Window

15	4	5	10
11	2	8	7
13	3	16	1
9	14	12	6

Page 123: Just Your Type

11	14	12	2
7	9	1	15
4	16	6	13
10	3	8	5

Page 124: Pattern Mixing No. 1 (A2): One stitch really stands out. No. 2 (B2): A checkerboard design has rotated slightly. No. 3 (B3 to B4): One orange stripe has thickened. No. 4 (B4): The black pattern on the red rug has edited its ending. No. 5 (C2): Four new triangles equals one great new look. No. 6 (C4): Isn't something missing in the center of that diamond? No. 7 (C5): The geometric shapes in one line of the pattern have gone completely yellow. No. 8 (D2): Another diagonally striped rectangle wove its way into that rug. No. 9 (D3): Is someone pulling strings here? No. 10 (D4): One more tassel's been tacked on. No. 11 (E2): There's less sun creeping through the entryway. No. 12 (E3): A green vertical stripe has vanished.

Page 126: The Plane Truth No. 1 (A3): Seeing double? Nos. 2 and 3 (A4): A drawer's hole has moved to the right. And a label has scooted up. Nos. 4 and 5 (A5): The plane earned a second star. And just outside, two bricks have gone vertical. No. 6 (B1): The gauge has moved. Maybe we've been taken on a ride into the danger zone. No. 7 (B2): Ah, so it's a *two*-seater. No. 8 (B3): His handsome earflap picked up a snap. No. 9 (B4 to C4): The wing's cross is now fully outlined. No. 10 (C1): The drill press handle's been pushed. Good thing he's got those sweet goggles. Nos. 11 and 12 (C2): The antenna is now two-pronged. And two copies of one book? No wonder it's a best-seller. No. 13 (C3): His sleeve is covering his watch. No. 14 (C5): The plane's fuselage is bluer. Nos. 15 and 16 (D4): That drawer handle's gotten heftier, while the cabinet has been refaced (looking smooth, too). No. 17 (D5): The flap on the wing has gotten longer. No. 18 (E1): The jigsaw's back edge now has a three-hole punch. No. 19 (E2): Now you C-clamp, now you don't. No. 20 (E3): The model picked up an extra white line.

[ANIMALS]

Page 130: Hang in There Nos. 1, 2, and 3 (C2): Poor little guy—can't smell a thing. As if that's not bad enough, one eye has rotated. And could someone give him a hand—or at least find the one that's missing? No. 4 (C2 to C4): On the upside, he's such a fast hopper that he's got a racing stripe. No. 5 (C3): His belly seems to be even more yellow. (Better smile when you say that.) No. 6 (D2 to D3): His hand has gone greener. That should please Al Gore. No. 7 (D5): Lunch has arrived. No. 8 (E2): A drop of dew now drips from the leaf. No. 9 (E2 to E3): One leaf has been stripped. No. 10 (E4): Sorry, ladies—he's obviously spoken for.

Page 132: Unusual Suspects No. 1 (B1): That tiger's ears are a bit spotty. No. 2 (B3 to D3): Whoa, kitty-kitty. No. 3 (B4): Can you hare me now? No. 4 (B5): What's that monkey all snobbish about? No. 5 (C1): Hey, spotty ears, you lost some stripes! No. 6 (C3): The bandanna is a nice touch. No. 7 (C4): Who says a leopard can't change its spots? Well, one spot anyway. No. 8 (C5): The hills are alive—and growing. No. 9 (D5): We hope that a leopard's tail curls down when it's *happy*. No. 10 (E1): Even lions would think those dandelions are dandy.

Page 133: Finding Nemo No. 1 (A1): Does that fish know where it's going? No. 2 (A4): This guy is swimming up. No. 3 (B1): That little rock rolled away. No. 4 (B2): Are we seeing double or are there now two yellow fishes? No. 5 (B4): He's extra-stripy. No. 6 (B5): Don't give us that big fish-eye. No. 7 (C5): So what do you see down there? Nos. 8 and 9 (D1): Um, Mr. Frog? You might be in over your head. Meanwhile, the rock sure looks surprised. No. 10 (E3): That rock is much bigger.

Page 134: Pretty Snaky No. 1 (A1 to A2): The paint's been stripped from the wooden ledge. No. 2 (A1 to C1): Just how long *is* this serpent? No. 3 (A2 to B3): One red patch of skin has gone off the scales. No. 4 (A4): Bye-bye, black stripe. Nos. 5 and 6 (B5): The snake's nostrils have moved closer together, and the two black prongs on its head now meet and form a circle. No. 7 (C2): There's a hole in the leaf, dear Liza, dear Liza. No. 8 (D2): A white segment has fattened up. No. 9 (D3 to E4): A blade of grass has been mowed down. No. 10 (E1): Who turned over that new leaf? No. 11 (E3): Some herbivorous snacking has been going on here.

Page 136: Best in Show No. 1 (A5 to B5): The pole's been cut short. No. 2 (B1): Is that Hair in a Can? No. 3 (B1 to C1): We kind of liked the tie, frankly. No. 4 (B5): He's just puffing along. No. 5 (C2 to D2): Another well-dressed livestock fan has arrived. No. 6 (C3): That red is much livelier. No. 7 (C5): Looks like he's taking home the blue ribbon! No. 8 (D1): While we're being honest, the new kilt length? A bit matronly. No. 9 (D2): Those things multiply like rabbits. No. 10 (D3 to E3): Donkey's tail is quite luxurious. No. 11 (E2): He changed into gym socks. No. 12 (E5): Anyone for croquet?

Page 137: Can You Bear It? No. 1 (A3): Don't know what goes on behind those curtains, but the bus needed more ventilation. No. 2 (A3 to B4): And more curtains. No. 3 (B1): The door handle has moved. No. 4 (B4 to C4): The bowl on his back has bounced to the other side. Nos. 5 and 6 (C3): His bag's got a new logo. And *there's* the bear's other ear. No. 7 (C5 to D5): This guy's leg has gotten longer. No. 8 (D2): His shoe can now be seen. No. 9 (E5): The curb has added a paving stone. **Did you find the secret bonus difference?** If not, log on to *www.LIFE.com* to find out what it is.

Page 138: One Big Fowl-up

2	6	7
1	8	4
9	3	5

Page 139: Scrambled Eggs

6	4	9
8	2	1
3	7	5

Page 140: Flying the Coop No. 1 (B1): The roof is trending upward. No. 2 (B2): Solving this puzzle might hinge on those hinges. No. 3 (B5): Her sweater dropped a diamond. No. 4 (C3): Hey, you—stop peeking and start pecking. Nos. 5 and 6 (C4): The feed bowl's been topped off. And her sweater's detail has really gone beyond the fringe. No. 7 (C5): What's that in the back? Chicken run! No. 8 (D3 to D4): SHACK is no longer underscored. Nos. 9 and 10 (E1): One bird's dark neck feathers have multiplied. And it's time for that other one to stretch her legs, apparently.

Page 141: Trunk Show Nos. 1 and 2 (A4): He's got a point—a much bigger point, in fact. And someone's got a bird's-eye view. No. 3 (B1): When in Rome, wear headgear like the Romans did. No. 4 (B2): The elephant on the flag packed light! (He left his trunk at home.) No. 5 (B3): His new look is super-stripy. No. 6 (C2): This pachyderm's headdress is red-less. No. 7 (C4 to C5): That onion-shaped decoration has really sprouted. No. 8 (D2 to D3): The red blanket is more ornate. No. 9 (D4): One tusk has grown. No. 10 (D5): How do *you* spell "elephant"? No. 11 (E2): We just love your nails!

Page 142: Home Stretch No. 1 (A1): More clouds have rolled in. No. 2 (B3 to B4): *Love* the new lashes. Couldn't love them more. No. 3 (C1): Oh, hush up, you. No. 4 (C2): Look over there! No. 5 (C5): That guy wins by a neck. No. 6 (D2): Hey, where did old what's-his-name go? No. 7 (D3): Talk about political bias—that ostrich totally leans to the left. No. 8 (D4): Who's the new guy? No. 9 (E1): There's a rebel in every crowd (or herd). No. 10 (E5): He's got a winning smile.

Page 144: Stumped Yet? No. 1 (A2): One lady has leaped leftward. No. 2 (A4 to B5): Her new look has made her dotty. No. 3 (B3): Who's the new gal? Nos. 4 and 5 (C2): One little bug doesn't look like it's from around here. And one left town. No. 6 (C3): An about-face? That's a bit buggy. No. 7 (C4): Another crevice in the wood? Groovy! No. 8 (C5 to E5): The black hole has been filled in. No. 9 (D1 to E1): Do ladybugs like grass? No. 10 (E3): Not to put you on the spot, ma'am, but you've got a huge dot on your back.

[LIFE CLASSICS]

Page 148: Ground Control No. 1 (A3 to A4): An extra wire should keep events current. No. 2 (B1): Soil study is a dirty business—better stock up on paper towels. Nos. 3 and 4 (B3): A second knob has appeared on the scope, and the eyepiece has been extended, to take the long view. No. 5 (B4): It's a black-tie affair. No. 6 (C2): A sample's been sealed. No. 7 (C2 to C4): Australia and Venezuela have switched places. Wait till Rand McNally hears that. No. 8 (C3): Another stack of samples has been collected. No. 9 (D2): Here's a

recap: The container's been covered. No. 10 (E1): How do you turn a country into a sentence? Change IRAN to I RAN. No. 11 (E5): Bull's-eye!

Page 150: **Odds and Ends** No. 1 (B1): One bottle now has a fruit topping. No. 2 (B2 to C2): Must be the 2-liter bottle of chemicals. No. 3 (C1): Fetch that bone before it rolls away! No. 4 (C2): Some fluid has a darker hue. No. 5 (C3): Is that starfish waving? No. 6 (C5): Is that the skull of a *Homo vampirus*? No. 7 (D2): There seems to be an attraction between two samples. No. 8 (D3): Four boxes are better than three. No. 9 (D4): Where are those critters headed now? No. 10 (E3): Two disks have switched places. No. 11 (E5): A beaker has lost its markings.

Page 152: **Signs Are Good** No. 1 (B1 to B2): The demand for electricity has increased. No. 2 (B3): The light pole's neck has stretched out. Nos. 3 and 4 (C2): Gee, those *G*'s look different. And we see another chimney has popped up. No. 5 (C5 to D5): The sign's gap has been closed. No. 6 (D1): That car may be closer than it appears. Nos. 7 and 8 (D3): The pole position has changed. And are you sure that light is properly grounded? No. 9 (D5): That's no longer a cent symbol.

Page 153: **Go to Town** No. 1 (A2): One window's been repainted. No. 2 (A5): Looks like gas is rising again. Or at least the Esso sign is. No. 3 (B1): A white sign front has lengthened. No. 4 (C1): The meter grew taller. No. 5 (C3): Stripes? That's so racy. No. 6 (C4): Is he flashing his brights at that tractor? No. 7 (C5): Guess she changed her mind. No. 8 (D3): You lose a hubcap, buddy? No. 9 (D3 to D5): Please cross at the crosswalk. No. 10 (D4): How exhausting—the tractor's pipes have flip-flopped. No. 11 (E1): Nice paint job!

Page 154: **They're Playing Our Song** No. 1 (A1): Please turn around, sir. No. 2 (A2): Someone lose a set of black keys? No. 3 (A4): Now we'll never know what the right hand's doing. No. 4 (A5): One of these ruffians must have smashed a window. No. 5 (B2): Some notes have been passed to the right. No. 6 (B3): The sheet music is higher. Maybe he's an alto. No. 7 (C2): A teaching aid has been twinned. No. 8 (C5): Now there are enough books for everyone. No. 9 (D1): Thanks to the teacher's hot medley, the desks have melded. No. 10 (D1 to E1): Her headband has lightened up. No. 11 (D4): Her keyboard has stretched out—perfect for playing extended versions. No. 12 (D5): His collar got collared. **Did you find the secret bonus difference?** If not, log on to *www.LIFE.com* to find out what it is.

Page 156: **Construction Sight** No. 1 (A2): The dirt just keeps piling up, doesn't it? No. 2 (A4): Someone tell the new guy to get busy. No. 3 (B2): Oh, goody—an extra cabinet. No. 4 (C2): One burner has burned out.

Nos. 5 and 6 (C3): The crate has an extra board's support, while the fridge handle is now turned down. No. 7 (C4): The loo is larger. Nos. 8, 9, and 10 (D3): The bags are really stacking up, the tub's tag has rotated, and doesn't everyone love exposed plumbing? No. 11 (E1): Someone straightened the wood stack. No. 12 (E3 to E4): What a ton of bricks!

Page 157: **Lawn and Order** No. 1 (A4 to A5): There's been an arboreal growth spurt. No. 2 (C1): He's outta here! Nos. 3 and 4 (C4): Who was expecting twins? And please button up your overcoat, m'lady. Nos. 5 and 6 (C5): Have a seat. Plus, that sure is a mighty big bow for such a little lady. No. 7 (D2): Baby's turned away from the sun. Fear of freckles, perhaps. Nos. 8 and 9 (D4): Sir, is that your real hair? Meanwhile, Junior has pulled up his socks. No. 10 (E1 to E2): His tie has grown longer.

Page 158: **Stay on Track** No. 1 (A2 to B2): *Tim-berrrr!* No. 2 (A3): That flag has doubled down. No. 3 (B1 to C1): Is that new horse playing chicken? No. 4 (B3): Hats off to this horsey! No. 5 (B4): It's extra-post time for that roof. No. 6 (C1 to D1): His recipe for winning calls for two cups. No. 7 (C2): His hatband is a fatband. No. 8 (D1): The potted plant is shrinking. No. 9 (D5): One ribbon is longer. No. 10 (E3 to E4): The shadow has crept forward. Why? Only the shadow knows.

Page 160: **Hammer Time** No. 1 (A1): A little to the left, boys. No. 2 (B2): He's tipped his hat to you (for doing these puzzles so well). No. 3 (B4): Does that shadow know something we don't? No. 4 (B5): Special delivery! No. 5 (C2): His hammer must have slipped. No. 6 (D1): The doorway's been vacated. No. 7 (D2): She's shifted her paddle. No. 8 (E1 to E2): Watch your step! No. 9 (E4): He's hiked up his trousers. No. 10 (E5): The lumber is longer.

Page 162: **Read Any Good Books Lately?** No. 1 (A1 to B1): What a major bust he turned out to be. Nos. 2 and 3 (A3): The Grecian urn now has EZ-grip handles. Which someone apparently thinks is kind of shady. No. 4 (A4): The candles in the reflection are no longer mirror images. No. 5 (B2): That chandelier is burning at both ends. No. 6 (B3): A wall motif has been repeated. Tastefully, of course. No. 7 (B4): This sconce has stretched. No. 8 (C1): A book's been checked out. No. 9 (C2): Get a load of that figurine. Hubba-hubba. No. 10 (C3): No tie required? Doesn't anyone dress for dinner anymore? No. 11 (C4): The sculpture has lost its reflection. No, it's not a vampire. No. 12 (D1): More white volumes have been shelved. No. 13 (D4 to D5): That chair's new armrest doesn't sit too well with us. No. 14 (E2): Fido's fur is looking patchy. No. 15 (E3 to E4): Another black tile has been laid down. And now this book must be, too.